The
Inflection
Election

ALSO BY MARK GREEN

Wrecking America: How Trump's Lawbreaking & Lies Betray All
(w/ Ralph Nader, 2020)

Fake President: Decoding Trump's Gaslighting & Corruption (w/ Ralph Nader, 2019)

Bright Infinite Future: A Generational Memoir on the Progressive Rise (2016)

Change for America: Progressive Blueprints for the 44th President
(ed. w/ M. Jolin, 2009)

Losing our Democracy (2006)

Defend Yourself: How to Protect Your Health, Money and Rights (2006)

What We Stand For: A Program for Progressive Patriotism (ed., 2004)

The Book on Bush: How George W. (Mis)Leads America (w/ Eric Alterman, 2004)

Selling Out: How Big Corporate Money Buys Elections . . . and Betrays Our Democracy (2002)

Mark Green's Guide to Coping in New York City (2000)

The Consumer Bible (w/ Nancy Youman, 1998)

Changing America: Blueprints for the New Administration (ed., 1993)

America's Transition: Blueprints for the 1990s (ed. w/ Mark Pinsky, 1989)

Reagan's Reign of Error: The Instant Nostalgia Edition (w/ Gail MacColl, 1987)

The Challenge of Hidden Profits: Reducing Corporate Bureaucracy
(w/ John Berry, 1985)

Winning Back America (1982)

The Big Business Reader (ed. w/ Robert Massie Jr., 1980)

Taming the Giant Corporation (w/ Ralph Nader & Joel Seligman, 1976)

The Other Government: The Unseen Power of Washington Lawyers (1975)

Corporate Power in America (ed. w/ Ralph Nader)

Verdicts on Lawyers (ed. w/ Ralph Nader,1976)

The Monopoly Makers (ed. 1973)

The Closed Enterprise System (w/ Beverly Moore Jr. & Bruce Wasserstein, 1972)

Who Runs Congress? (editions in 1972, 1975, 1979, 1984)

With Justice for Some (ed. w/ Bruce Wasserstein 1970)

The
Inflection
Election
Democracy or
Fascism in 2024?

by Mark Green
Foreword Rep. Jamie Raskin

Skyhorse Publishing

Skyhorse Publishing books may be purchased in bulk at special discounts
for sales promotion, corporate gifts, fund-raising, or educational purposes.
Special editions can also be created to specifications. For details, contact
the Special Sales Department, Skyhorse Publishing, 307 West 36th Street,
11th Floor, New York, NY 10018 or info@skyhorsepublishing.com.

Skyhorse and Skyhorse Publishing are registered trademarks of Skyhorse
Publishing, Inc., a Delaware corporation.

Visit our website at www.skyhorsepublishing.com.
Please follow our publisher Tony Lyons on Instagram @tonylyonsisuncertain

10 9 8 7 6 5 4 3 2 1

Library of Congress Cataloging-in-Publication Data is available on file.

Cover design by David Ter-Avanesyan
Cover images: Presidents by Getty Images, White House by Shutterstock

Print ISBN: 978-1-5107-8083-5
Ebook ISBN: 978-1-5107-8084-2

Printed in the United States of America

Toward a 'Bright Infinite Future' for Ava, Otis,
Moses & Josephine

CONTENTS

FOREWORD

BY REP. JAMIE RASKIN

I n *The Inflection Election*, Mark Green captures the central and irrevocable importance of the 2024 presidential election and depicts in fine-grained detail the choice that Americans now face.

On one path, we can choose to continue our national experiment in democratic freedom with all the necessary complications of democracy and freedom. We can stay true to the rule of law under the Constitution; we can defend the rights and liberties of the people; we can hold fast to the principle that the government as an entity must be an instrument to advance the well-being and common good of the whole society.

On the other path, even after everything we know about Donald Trump, his dangerous movement and his sordidly corrupt business model, we can choose to carry the country back into more of his trademark chaos, dysfunction, and authoritarianism. We could restore to office Trump's one sincere conviction: that the government is nothing but an instrument of personal self-enrichment, self-aggrandizement, and wealth maximization for the guy who lies, cheats, and steals his way into executive power and office.

Green's book is first about the dark path. It shows how Trump and his followers have created the kind of authoritarian movement that becomes fascism, mirroring and enabling the hard-right turn that autocratic leaders are taking all over the world.

From Russia to China, from Hungary to the Philippines, and from Venezuela to India, the autocrats and dictators are on the march. Using what twentieth-century Hungarian politician Matyos Rakosi called "salami tactics," they work to shave off thick slices of constitutional democracy to cement their total power over society.

For authoritarian politicians and movements, elections present both a rich opportunity for demagogic (or "populist," if you prefer) scapegoating inside the arena and a target for institutional vilification and destruction from the outside.

The autocrats, who have a deep personal sense of entitlement to rule, presumptively cast doubt on the integrity of democratic elections and then refuse to accept the outcome of any election that doesn't go their way. In 2020 Joe Biden beat Trump by more than seven million votes, 306-232 in the electoral college, but Trump's carefully crafted Big Lie—rejected in sixty federal and state court cases across the land—set the stage for his efforts to sabotage the election and simply seize the presidency. This lawless power grab culminated in the convergence of Trump's backroom "self-coup," as the political scientists call it, with a violent and bloody mob insurrection on January 6, 2021. It then morphed into passage by Trump's party of over sixty restrictive voting laws and nineteen election interference laws in the states to further entrench obstruction of democracy.

Authoritarians of this type gleefully embrace and encourage political violence to terrorize their political opponents and chill dissent. And we have seen a lot of that. All of these fascistic tactics are used to elevate the will of a charismatic leader above the rule of law, the Constitution, and basic political morality.

Because we are still in the middle of the crisis, it is important to diagnose our beleaguered condition. I remember a time when it was both unnecessary and impolite to use the word "fascism" in American politics. Today it is essential. Fascists gain and retain power through propaganda, disinformation, scapegoating, mob violence, alliances with foreign dictators and despots, and the theft or conversion of public resources for private gain.

But Green's fine book, an urgent twenty-first-century democratic pamphlet, also shows us what it would mean to choose well and get back on the bright path too. He contrasts Donald Trump's selfish lust for power not only with the ideals of freedom and democracy that the American people have fought to realize in our history but with the positive public agenda available to us now.

Green describes the opportunity that we have to build an economy that works for everyone, not just the plutocrats and kleptocrats, and to welcome participation by people of every background into a vibrant pluralist democracy. He builds an admirable case for a "New Patriotism" that will help us stand our ground instead of running scared from the MAGA bullies and billionaires.

This fine book is an essential primer about the stakes of the momentous 2024 election. We owe Mark Green a debt of gratitude for making the intuitively obvious explicitly clear to everyone.

INTRODUCTION
"YOU. CANNOT. BE. SERIOUS!"

I think when the history of this period is written, our children and our grandchildren will ask, "What were you doing when our House of Democracy was on fire?"
—Sen. Rafael Warnock

April 19, 2025

WASHINGTON (AP)—*At the direction of Donald Trump, the forty-seventh president of the United States, Attorney General Ken Paxton yesterday sent teams of FBI agents to the residences of Rachel Maddow, General Mark Milley, and Hillary Clinton.*

Knocking on their doors at precisely 9 a.m., the lead agents were polite but firm, all identically telling their targets, "We've come to confiscate your electronic devices pursuant to a lawful warrant. You are not now under arrest."

Clinton appeared to be the most calm and least surprised. "What might the charges be?"

"Sorry, ma'am," said the female agent with a small ponytail and large vest emblazoned with the familiar oversized yellow letters FBI. "We're not allowed to say."

Within the hour, Democratic senators Elizabeth Warren and Cory Booker issued a joint statement calling the actions "obviously revenge prosecutions—we did not defeat fascism abroad in 1945 in order to imitate it eighty years later at home."

At the Department of Homeland Security, Secretary Stephen Miller hit back. "May we remind the senators that the American people have spoken?" an apparent reference to Trump's electoral vote victory of 271 to 269, despite Biden winning the popular vote margin by ten million votes over Trump—or 48 percent to 40 percent. (The remaining 12 percent went to four minor-party candidates.)

The electoral college, however, for the third time in the last seven presidential elections, turned a popular vote victory into a narrow loss.

In a wide-ranging interview with Newsmax, *Miller also made news on immigration. "Today, we're beginning construction of 50,000 modular homes in Waco, Texas to launch 'Operation Relocation' to deport three million Americans who came here illegally. Promise made. Promise kept."*

Yesterday afternoon, the Pentagon sent in federal troops under the 1871 KKK Insurrection Act to a dozen cities holding "Democracy, Not Dictatorship" signs—organized by Black Lives Matter and MoveOn. Thousands of peaceful protestors in each location appeared shocked to see M1 Abrams tanks rolling down streets to block their paths with tear gas, flash grenades, and rubber bullets. Thirteen students were killed in Atlanta alone when they stood in front of tanks that wouldn't stop.

Reporters caught up with President Trump early afternoon in between rounds of golf at his Bedminster Club. "Well, nothing new here—didn't Biden do the same thing to me and Rudy? Sorry about those deaths in Atlanta but, excuse me, what were those pro-testors doing in front of our tanks? Anyway, it could have been a lot worse, right? And please remember that today is the exact 250th anniversary of the battles of Lexington and Concord that began our journey as an exceptional model of Freedom and Democracy."

* * *

In 2006, my book *Losing Our Democracy* warned of an American democracy in slow decline. Four years ago I wrote several articles about how Trump and MAGA were becoming increasingly fascistic . . . to widespread yawns. And during the 2022 midterms, Ralph Nader and I—along with twenty-four progressive authors—released a lengthy monograph entitled *Crushing the GOP* to suggest phrasing and framing to help reduce expected losses.

But if earlier warnings about creeping fascism struck some as naive, it would now be willfully stupid to ignore Trump's catch-me-if-you-can Caesarism . . . especially after declaring his desire to be a "Day One Dictator" (like he'd voluntarily stop after twenty-four hours), vowing to destroy foreign and liberal "vermin . . . poisoning the blood of our country," promising to criminally prosecute political opponents, defending a presidential immunity to kill-at-will, and rounding up millions of undocumented immigrants into "camps" before deporting them and their families. "This is who he is," concluded Trump-biographer Maggie Haberman.

We are now all watching a reality-TV sequel to Rachel Maddow's bestselling 2023 book, *Prequel: An American Fight Against Fascism*, about an attempt in the 1940s to sabotage the

American Experiment during wartime. While that fight failed, the script for the Trump finale has not yet been written.

Obviously, Trump is not the genocidal German chancellor from Kristallnacht in 1938 to his suicide in April 1945. Only Hitler was Hitler. But it's also disingenuous to deny a rhetorical resemblance to the 1920s fanatic who failed and was jailed for a year following his unsuccessful 1923 Beer Hall insurrection (which curiously also left seven dead, as did January 6) to overthrow the Weimar Republic. After he had served a year and was released, the *New York Times* on December 21, 1924, actually ran this headline, "Hitler Tamed by Prison." The article ended on the bright note that "it is believed he will retire to private life in Austria, the country of his birth."

At that time, he was considered a demagogic clown by leading politicians, much like Trump before his election in 2016 and after his loss in 2020. Looking back now, what should we make of both Donald's and his first wife Ivana's admissions that he kept a volume of Hitler's speeches in a cabinet by their bed?

* * *

Denial is instinctual—who doesn't think, as a car crash is unfolding, *This can't be happening!* Then *BOOM!*

Director James Cameron called his film *Titanic* "a great novel that really happened." Trumpism is also fantastic yet now really happening as well. While millions of voters and much of the mainstream media stay in their politics-as-usual cocoons despite all his threats and trials, Donald J. Trump is as plausibly hopeful of going back to the White House as he is fearful of going to prison, and relishes cheating his banks, wives, voters,

Trump "University" students, own lawyers, and golf scores. Even unhinged hints that Gen. Milley deserves execution for treason have been met with silence or shrugs by Republican officeholders who routinely capitulate to his pathologies as ransom for power.

"He tells it like it is." Paul Noth/*The New Yorker*

None of that is new or news—Roy Cohn's protégé continues to shock but no longer surprise. What is unprecedented is that 2024 is becoming an inflection election between a Party of Progress and a Party of Dangerous Extremists—not one miscreant but a whole swath of accomplices who are either "proud MAGAs or scared MAGAs," in the insight of Marc C. Elias, founder of the Democracy Docket. As subsequent chapters elaborate, one side embraces popular government in pursuit of the common good while the other—the progeny of Joe McCarthy,

William F. Buckley Jr., Father Coughlin, Richard Nixon, Ronald Reagan, Rush Limbaugh, Newt Gingrich, Sarah Palin, Steve Bannon and, of course, Donald Trump—has formed a political base that darkly hints of a new Civil War.

As of Spring 2024, neither team has a prohibitive advantage. There are too many jury verdicts, ongoing wars, possible third-party candidates, Supreme Court reversals of "settled" precedent, gun massacres, and "October Surprises" to go. But the stakes are no mystery.

> *"Inflection Point:* "A critical point at which a major or decisive change takes place."
>
> —Dictionary.com

If Republicans should somehow run the table this November—with a revanchist Supreme Court already in its column—a minority of Americans could cancel a century of progress and make the world's oldest democracy no longer democratic. For the founders never anticipated a future leader who would say "I don't debate my opponents, I destroy them."

Oh, sorry—that wasn't Donald Trump but Benito Mussolini in 1936. Notice, however, how easy it was to confuse these two swaggering strongmen. "What we are seeing," said Gen. Barry McCaffery on national TV in late 2023, "is a parallel to the 1930s . . . and a major threat to the United States."

The evidence? Let's connect their dots. Most Republicans repeat Trump's two Biggest Lies—viz., that he won the 2020 election and that all his felony indictments result from hundreds of partisan prosecutors, grand juries, and judges magically collaborating. Then, as if those two world-class whoppers and "vermin" weren't enough, Speaker Mike Johnson's GOP Caucus is now flagrantly proving that they range all the way from the Far-Right to the Further-Right. Consider MAGA's cornerstones:

- *Implied racism*: "White Christian Nationalism, the Great Replacement Theory, Critical Race Theory" add up to "criminalizing being Black," in the view of Ruth Ben-Ghiat, a scholar of authoritarianism. The unspoken message to its base is, "don't worry, everything will be all white."
- *Hateful language* has triggered thousands of death threats and numerous acts of organized and loner violence (see chapter 3, "The MAGA Mobocracy," and chapter 5, "Loathe Thy Neighbor").
- *Pardons or praise* for 1,200 insurrectionists convicted of crimes.
- *Massive voter suppression of Democrats* (rebranded as "voter integrity").
- *Big-Brother bans* on abortions, books, drag shows, and marriage equality—what they call, without any sense of irony, their "Freedom Agenda."
- *Climate denialism* despite rising and record heat, wildfires, and flooding.
- *Vaccine denialism* that has needlessly cost over 300,000 Americans their lives (disproportionately anti-vax libertarians, which is not only immoral but pretty foolish for a party of libertarians).

- *Kudos for dictators and killers* such as Vladimir Putin, Xi Jinping, Kim Jong Un, even "very smart" Hamas (according to Trump) but never praise of America's allies.
- *Contempt for the free media* whom Trump repeatedly calls, echoing Stalin's ominous phrase "enemies of the people."

There must be a word that summarizes such fringeworthy talk, but it sure isn't "conservative" in the way Eisenhower, Reagan, or the Bushes would have understood it. This is extremism posing as patriotism. One emotionally satisfying response to Republicans who "create their own reality" (Karl Rove's phrase) might be to simply quote the familiar rage of tennis great John McEnroe, *"You. Cannot. Be. Serious!"* It's frankly wearying and demeaning to engage with people as ignorant, cynical, or malicious as Lauren Boebert, Stephen Miller, and Lindsay Graham . . . but given the scale of their threats, indifference is not an option. Even debating people of such bad faith seems as useful as spooning out the ocean since, to quote the *New Yorker*'s Jelani Cobb, they "lie exponentially while fact-checkers respond arithmetically."

Instead, electorally smashing such an anti-American movement is the only sure way to return to a healthy two-party system where losers respect the choice of voters, like in the good old days of 1789–2016.

* * *

Most commentators are skeptical about this prospect due to a Senate map heavily tilted to red state contests (by twenty-three to ten) and the GOP's nearly sole focus on "negative partisanship." Nor is it reasonable to expect that Republican leaders may finally rebuke Trump when they refused that very opportunity at the critical moment in both Senate impeachment trials.

But as Norman Cousins noted a half century ago, "no one is smart enough to be a pessimist." A handful of off-cycle elections over the past two years in purple jurisdictions show the possibilities. In each of seven state referendums to legalize abortion, the pro-abortion side easily won. In a Wisconsin statewide race to determine whether its state Supreme Court lurched Left or Right, a progressive judicial candidate won by a jaw-dropping 11 percentage points; in Michigan, a few point swing helped to easily reelect a Democratic governor and supportive majorities in both legislative chambers for the first time in decades. Then last February, Tom Suozzi easily won back his NY-03 seat on Long Island.

Are these aberrations or harbingers for 2024?

"It's too soon to tell" as Zhou Enlai famously said when asked in the 1970s about the influence of the French Revolution. But we do know that election deniers flopped at the polls in the final month of the 2022 midterm elections. According to a survey by the nonprofit States United Action, "culture war" issues—especially the Court's *Dobbs* decision overturning *Roe v. Wade*—helped boost Democrats on average 2.3–3.7 points to hold the Senate and avoid a blowout in the House. Yet there's little evidence that sincerely oblivious MAGAs will soon slow their Pickett's Charge against basic American values, as that failed thrust against entrenched Union troops ended the decisive Battle of Gettysburg.

Possible outcomes consequently now stretch all the way from a narrow GOP takeover of the federal government by the holy alliance of this President, Speaker, and High Court . . . to a "Blue Backlash." Watergate, of course, spurred huge Democratic gains in 1974—a reprise is now feasible due to several trends with the combined potential, concluded a glum Governor Chris Sununu (R-NH), of sinking many Republican candidates up and down the ballot.

Let's put aside those Cassandras obsessing over a third-year slump for Biden, which was not unlike other incumbent presidents seeking reelection with problematic economies, including Truman, Carter, Reagan, Clinton, Obama, and Trump. (Four won.) No one has been more convincing how polls are not votes and how Democrats have been consistently outperforming speculation than analyst Simon Rosenberg (@SimonWDC). And no better Twitter handle on '24 than LOLGOP.

As in all elections, there's a positive and a negative case for Democrats in 2024:

I. THE POSITIVE

- America has a **more progressive electorate**, according to pollster Celinda Lake. Since 2016, twenty million older Americans have died, while thirty million younger voters now comprise a Gen Z with its keen generational concern over climate, guns, COVID, and racial and gender justice, as well as growing up in the zeitgeist of Obama's success and Trump's havoc. In the most recent elections, eighteen- to twenty-nine-year-olds have broken over 60 percent for Democrats. David Leonhardt of the *New York Times* called this

development "one of the biggest stories in American
politics and a major advantage for the Democratic
party." Indeed, this generation will be the first to have
a majority-minority population throughout all their
voting lives, which is a problem for the party of the
Far-White.*

- The Biden Administration has **a record of economic
  revival and kitchen-table successes** after the
  pandemic and Trumponomics. (When incumbent
  Jimmy Carter lost in 1980, the "Misery Index"
  [joblessness and inflation] stood at 20; today it's under
  seven.) After years of being in the doldrums, organized
  labor is enjoying a surge in popularity following a series
  of successful strikes. Pretty hard to see those folks on
  the UAW picket lines voting for a nominee with a gold-
  plated toilet. Not to mention that there's an emerging
  conventional wisdom, as reflected in a January
  Washington Post headline "Falling Inflation, Rising
  Growth, Give U. S. the World's Best Recovery," that will
  presumably undercut GOP economic lamentations that
  "the sky keeps falling."

But more than good news is needed when one party—and its
cable sidekick—spew daily calumnies while the other is headed

---

* In the immediate aftermath of the Hamas-Israeli War, surveys indicated that
while a significant majority of all Americans favored Israel, a very different majority of younger voters did not, with Biden's favorable ratings taking a hit with them.
Without politically weighing this continuing conflict further, it's unlikely that it will
prove decisive a year after it began against a xenophobic Republican like Trump,
an admittedly speculative conclusion.

by *The Last Politician* (Frank Foer's smart book title), a president whose superpower is his experience, empathy, and equanimity. Although periodically denouncing Trumpian assaults on democracy and decency—"You can't be pro-Insurrection and pro-Democracy"—Biden throughout 2023 usually adopted a presidential persona that avoided contemporary rebuttals in vernacular language.

On the one hand, that smartly sustained the usual respect accorded residents of the White House and avoided bottom-feeders who revel in mud wrestling. But that also ran the risk that smears stick, as happened after John Kerry's initial reluctance in 2004 to challenge "Swift Boat" veterans lying about his exemplary service record. But once Trump not only became the de facto nominee in January but also his hysterical responses to worsening legal jeopardy grew, so did the sharpness and frequency of Biden and Harris's rejoinders.

When it comes to the music of politics, Republicans still have a bigger beat, and Democrats better lyrics. On that score—and reflecting the angst of influential radio-host Charlamagne tha God, "Trump sounds more sincere telling lies than Biden does telling the truth"—Team Biden could use help with more memorable messaging. Allies and surrogates—who @SimonWDC called "information warriors"—can provide backup to keep elected Democrats on offense and Trumpists on the ropes . . . not because this or any author has the "best words" but because all of us know more than any of us.

II. THE NEGATIVE

- The prospect that **a serial criminal will head the Fall GOP ballot** should elevate corruption to a top-tier issue. Recall that Trump in 2016 said that a mere FBI investigation ought to disqualify Hillary Clinton. Some journalist needs to ask Trump how voters should regard ninety-one actual indictments and a conviction or two? And what could any GOP candidate say this fall if asked in a debate or interview: "How can you take an oath to uphold the Constitution when you support a person credibly accused of masterminding the greatest constitutional crime ever against our country?" In the view of David Frum in *The Atlantic,* "The government cannot function with an indicted or convicted criminal as its head. For his own survival, he would have to destroy the rule of law."

- Even beyond Trump's extensive rap sheet, **Republicans are a "Party of Corruption."** Harsh? Yes. True? Ethics is apparently not a top GOP issue when 67 percent of them say they would still vote for Trump if he were a convicted felon and when fair-minded people contrast the fifty-point difference between an indicted Sen. Bob Menendez falling to 10 percent of his reelection primary vote while ex-president Trump *rises* to 60 percent after his summer of indictments. How can Republican leaders explain that gap? (The answer "What about Hunter?" will not cut it.)

- An **"Extreme Court"**—which has lost a third of its popularity in the past three years, even prior to its Section III Disqualification decision—apparently can't stop trying to go in reverse while also ignoring ethics norms. This means making Justices Clarence Thomas

and Samuel Alito even more infamous, as Senator
Sheldon Whitehouse does best.

- The GOP agenda on **abortion, guns, and health care
  is far more extreme than mainstream**, especially
  given the furious and sustained backlash against
  the anti-abortion *Dobbs* decision in 2022 and the
  growing number of school shootings that frighten
  suburban moms, along with everyone else. And
  Trump's repeated vow to end Obamacare, which would
  make 54 million people with a preexisting condition
  basically uninsurable, seems to have been written by a
  Democratic operative disguised under a red hat.

- When it comes to **climate violence,** Republicans
  prefer silence since their GOP pockets are stuffed
  with campaign funds from fossil fools (see chapter
  7, "Un-Science"). Every summer seems to produce
  reports of the "hottest month ever," while the waters off
  Miami in August 2023 were officially deemed too hot
  for swimming.

- In the spirit of Truman's 1948 campaign against the
  "Do-Nothing Congress," Republicans are again **the
  party of grievance, not governance.** See how GOP
  House chairs Jim Jordan and James Comer have
  turned their committees' investigations into innuendo
  machines, not to mention that the GOP House in 2023
  enacted a total of twenty-seven laws, compared to
  350 in Pelosi's last year as speaker. GOP Rep. Chip
  Roy, a Freedom Caucus leader, shouted in frustration
  on the House floor, "I want my Republican colleagues
  to give me one thing that I can go campaign on and

say we did. *One!"* And when the Republican Party last
controlled the White House, Senate, and House in
2004, former senator Claire McCaskill reminds us,
"they did nothing about the deficit or border."

Those are pretty big headwinds for the already minority party,
notwithstanding Democratic political vulnerabilities over the
border, inflation, Middle East, and Biden's age. Nor is shouting
"woke" every third sentence about supposed cultural horrors
a winning rejoinder. Recall Gov. Ron DeSantis's spectacular
overreliance on it in his presidential bid. "We must fight the
woke in our schools. We must fight the woke in our businesses.
We must fight the woke in government agencies. We can never,
ever, surrender to woke." (See Insert II.) Despite the nice
rhythm, woke didn't work for him.

At the same time, skeptics who discount the power of metaphors and language should reflect on Churchill's trenchant
observation that "of all the talents bestowed upon men, none
is so precious as the gift of oratory. He who enjoys it wields a
power more durable than that of a great king." Among phrases
that indeed captured sentiment and shifted history: "Boston
Massacre" (thank you, Sam Adams), "A nation cannot exist
half-slave and half free," "A date which will live in infamy," "At
long last sir, have you no decency?", "We Shall Overcome," "I
have a dream," "Welfare Queen," "Willie Horton!" and, to be
honest, how "Stop The Steal" helped propagate that colossal
falsehood.

Rhetoric and narratives alone won't convert any significant
number of Trumpers in Cult 45 since their emotional devotion
to Donald has survived all his flagrant bullying and graft. For

deep-seated psychological reasons, most of the Republican base merge their identities with his chesty personality. Expecting a different result would be like convincing Boston Red Sox fans to buy Yankees season tickets.

Instead, opponents will have to focus on inspiring turnout of low-propensity voting Democrats and try to chip away up to a tenth of swing voters about what it would mean to their wallets and rights if Team Trump won the White House and Congress—increased taxes on the middle class, even more guns and gun deaths, higher drug prices, rural hospitals losing essential federal assistance, wider book bans, Black and gay friends suffering discrimination, and journalist pals indicted or incarcerated (some doctors too). There's really no bottom since a politician who can't admit error and delights in "doubling down" is, by that definition, always testing how low he can go—to paraphrase Daniel Patrick Moynihan, this year that means "Defining Democracy Down." (Admittedly, it's hard to go lower than Trump's "immunity claims" that would allow him to assassinate rivals without punishment.)

> *Not talking about fascism can make it easier for it to occur and to recur.*
> —Tracey Barrett, teacher in Asheville, North Carolina

Will such a radical program seem unpatriotic for those swing voters in up to ten swing states (especially Georgia, Michigan, Pennsylvania, and Wisconsin, as well as North Carolina, Virginia, Minnesota, Colorado, Arizona, and Nevada) who'll essentially draft the next chapter in the story of America?

* * *

The approaching election is coming into focus. If all the previous dots were aggregated into a pointillist painting, the portrait would resemble Orbán far more than Obama. Are voters comfortable with that kind of soft authoritarianism? Will they end up caring more about Biden's age or the longevity of democracy? Could 2024 be another 1974 when disgusted voters massively rejected the corruption of Nixon or another 2016 when a string of flukes narrowly sent a lifelong confidence man to the Oval Office? Is it really conceivable that a freedom-loving nation born after an heroic rebellion against the mighty British monarch would *elect* one 234 years later?

Last, the reality of an *Inflection Election* applies not just to the United States but the world as well. Authoritarian leaders like those in China, Russia, Iran, Hungary, Italy and Denmark will be watching closely on election night, as well as other nations concerned whether they're next to be contaminated by disinformation and extremism. One analyst in a Moscow-aligned think tank ominously predicted that 2024 "could be the year when the West's liberal elites lose control of the world order."

CHAPTER 1
FREEDOM . . . FOR WHOM?

I don't want to die because of Mike Johnson's religious views of abortion.
— **Molly Jong-Fast**

Totalitarianism means saying things you don't believe because you're afraid of the response. Donald Trump has created a totalitarian party—it's his own Orwellian world.
— **Stuart Stevens**, advisor to five GOP presidential campaigns

When a former president of France was asked to use one word to define his country—whose motto originating in 1789 has been "Liberté, égalité, fraternité"—he chose "égalité." Now imagine asking an ex-American president, regardless of party, the same question about his country. Would not the answer likely instead be "freedom"?

But "freedom" for what and for whom? Martin Luther King Jr. thought of what it meant for Freedom Riders in 1962 who risked their lives by heading South to get the boot of Bull Connor off the necks of Black people. King wanted everyone to choose their own "pursuit of happiness," including how his children, as he wrote in his famous "Letter from a Birmingham Jail," would be as free as white children to go to "Funtown." And of course, the name of his crowning achievement in 1963 was the "March for Jobs and Freedom."

To Ronald Reagan, on the other hand, it meant freedom *from* an overbearing Occupational Safety and Health Administration (OSHA) and Internal Revenue Service (IRS) and the ability to strike it rich without apologies or expensive safety nets. Laissez was fair. Reagan's Inaugural Address pivoted around his assertion that "government is not the solution to the problem, it is the problem." In this context, the Republican Right's fictional heroes have been John Wayne and John Galt.

But such a cramped version of freedom assumes that government and society are engaged in a zero-sum game—where more government necessarily means less freedom. In fact, public government can expand personal freedom when capitalism gets oppressive or produces avoidable harm. It's not complicated—the Clean Air Act and auto safety laws helped millions of Americans avoid premature deaths, which obviously would have eliminated *all* their freedoms.

This foundational conflict has recurred throughout our history as federalism versus states' rights, from the Constitutional Convention to the war over slavery to the sixties struggle over the civil rights laws . . . and jurisprudentially in the century from *Dred Scott* to *Brown v. Board of Education*. The core question then and now is the same—should there be a national floor of universal rights that "equalizes all and binds all," in the words of a nineteenth-century jurist about the Bill of Rights, or are those decisions better made at the state and local levels? FDR or Ronald Reagan?

The fight over freedom has returned to center stage in 2024 for two reasons: first, given the rhetorical power of "freedom" tracing back to "The Cause" in 1776, each party now wants to own a word more popular than equality, justice, or capitalism; and second, GOP obsession with unpopular culture war issues has thrown the party of white religious nationalism on the defensive everywhere but bright-red districts.

Bottom line: if Republicans choose to run campaigns based on a Trump/DeSantis/Johnson father-knows-best approach to censorship of books, bodily rights, and the supremacy of theocracy, then it'll be a losing proposition. A choice between a cultural Stasi and Rev. King's dream that government and freedom should reinforce each other is one worth fighting and winning.

FREEDOM OF SPEECH

"Free Speech" is more popular than "book bans"—but apparently Ron DeSantis never got the memo. He decided early on to run a campaign combining the bullying style of Joe McCarthy with the intolerance of Carrie Nation and Anthony Comstock—the two most priggish, censorial crusaders of the late nineteenth century.

We've seen how this has ended up in the past. There were bonfires of books burned by Nazis, the pictures of which cannot be unseen by anyone who's read the history. Temperance societies helped enact Prohibition in the Eighteenth Amendment (only to be reversed in the Twenty-Second one). Various jurisdictions have banned *Lady Chatterley's Lover, Ulysses,* and George Carlin, among many others, as pornographic.

DeSantis's maiden effort was enactment of the so-called "Individual Freedom Act"—or what he referred to as the

"Anti-Woke Act." It aimed, in his words, "to prohibit schools and companies from leveling blame based on race or sex [or made to] feel guilt, anguish or any other psychological distress" from racial anxiety.

That may sound nice in theory but no interpretation of the First Amendment permits censorship based on the feelings of some readers or listeners—certainly not children, a standard that would prohibit almost all controversial speech—which the governor, a well-educated lawyer with a large law department at his service, surely knew. But since his motivation was not the old Constitution but the approaching election, here's what happened next:

- The poem that America's Poet Laureate Amanda Gorman recited at Biden's Inauguration was banned from a Miami Lakes elementary school after the objection of one parent. Moms for Liberty chapters have called for schools to ban or limit access to dozens of books for any mention of transgender or queer themes, including Khaled Hosseini's *The Kite Runner* and George M. Johnson's award-winning memoir *All Boys Aren't Blue*. One high school teacher said that harassment from far-right groups has only eroded her vulnerable students' sense of safety. "Bullying from a peer is one thing," she said. "But bullying from full-grown adults is out of this world." (And that opinion preceded the collapsed reputation of a moralizing Moms for Liberty when news broke about sexual three-ways among its leaders.)
- A graphic novel version of a book about Anne Frank was removed from an Indian River County school

library. Other school libraries removed *Catcher in the Rye, 1984, Atlas Shrugged,* and any book that had the word "gay" in its title or gay characters (one was banned because the author's last name was "Gay"!).

- The *Orlando Sentinel* took two full pages of tiny type to list all the 673 banned books in school libraries (and that's just for one urban area). The PEN organization reported that a record number of books were banned throughout the country in 2002 and that—like school shootings—they inspire copycats and more book bans.

- One continuing target was "critical race theory" (discussed in more detail in "Loathe Thy Neighbor"), which supposedly overemphasized "institutional racism" as a contributor to many social and economic problems in America. What was especially weird, for all the huffing and puffing, is that no Florida school was shown to teach it in early grades.

It's true that, as a matter of constitutional law, a handful of categories of pure speech are widely recognized as exceptions to First Amendment freedoms—like defamation, libel, child pornography, perjury, the solicitation of a conspiracy, witness tampering, gag orders in trials—but suppressing truthful history has never been included in a country whose Bill of Rights begins with free speech. Other than Republican primary voters, do most Americans really believe that Black children had to live with a "badge of inferiority" for generations yet now it would be too traumatic for white children merely to learn about it? After touring Germany, Trevor Noah observed how it treats bad history differently in class: "Hey, hope you understand. Germany and Hitler did this, You're not responsible because you weren't there. But since you're the future of Germany, it's your responsibility to make sure this doesn't happen again."

FREEDOM FROM HARM

What comes to mind when you hear the word "regulation"? Not freedom, certainly. Due to Republican and corporate propaganda over decades, it has become tantamount to "red tape . . . bureaucracy . . . big government . . . unintended consequences" in the minds of many, if not most, voters.

But that impression requires amnesia about how Upton Sinclair's *The Jungle* on adulterated food shocked the nation and led to the Food Safety Act in 1907; the drug thalidomide taken during pregnancy produced deformed babies and led to the 1962 Drug Safety Act to better assure the "efficacy and safety" of such drugs; and after chlorofluorocarbons in such mundane products like deodorant spray were found to be depleting the earth's one ozone layer necessary to protect life from the sun's rays, the federal government in 1992 banned it.

"Free enterprise" caused those harms and regulation ended them. (Saving the ozone layer and planet would seem to be big deals but are somehow omitted when the GOP pushes its war on regulation.) And while it's easy to belittle bureaucrats, remember that we assign regulators the hard job of fixing problems that the private market can't monetize.

To be sure, millions of consumers freely "voting" with their dollars in the private marketplace reflect individual choices . . .

but so do public elections leading to laws and regulations that promote, in a phrase from the Constitution, "the General Welfare." Hard to see why only private choices are legitimate but public ones aren't. The producer-consumer social contract aims to create a humane capitalism based on the theory that it's better to locate guardrails at the top of cliffs than ambulances below.

The debate historically on regulation, however, has not been a fair fight. It's been largely kidnapped by big companies, trade associations, and law firms assailing "overregulation" without feeling the need to offer serious evidence or analysis. Their debate tactic is repetitive assertions: *"Less Regulation = Better Economy."* Period. As if stating the slogan is proof enough.

On the other side are millions of individual consumers who, due to what economists call "the free rider effect"—when consumers gain without having to pay for something—basically don't organize to form countervailing lobbying groups since they'll benefit even if they don't. (Imagine if the estimated 4.2 million Americans who *didn't* die in auto crashes since 1965 due to federal law and local traffic rules today magically discovered their near-misses—what an unbeatable coalition they would form to press for safer cars and products generally. Every day auto executives know where their interests lie; these non-dead millions don't.)

Back in the real world, the tide on regulation in the 1960s turned after Chamber of Commerce lawyer Lewis Powell (whom Nixon later put on the Court) wrote an enormously influential private memo in 1971 to his clients on how to organize and finance opposition to consumer groups in general and Ralph Nader in particular. With important exceptions like the Dodd-Frank Banking Reform Act and Elizabeth Warren's Consumer Finance Protection Bureau, his strategy largely succeeded. An attempt to create a Consumer Protection Agency to provide advocacy within each Washington agency—at the cost of a nickel per consumer—was defeated in 1978 by an unprecedented level of business opposition based on the Powell model.

That template kept repeating throughout the 1980s, and Reagan, in addition, appointed people not so much to run agencies as immobilize them. "Don't just do something, stand there!" became an unofficial mantra for people like Anne Gorsuch at Reagan's EPA (yes the mother of Neil), forced to resign after too obviously weakening her own office. More recently, Trump used every possible excuse—like COVID—to try to avoid implementing existing laws and enacting new ones. Throughout his 2020 campaign, all he said on the subject of health/safety rules was to brag that he had eliminated eighty-two regulations, with not a word about benefits lost. A *New York Times* analysis of the regulations repealed or rolled back "could swiftly increase greenhouse gas emissions and to thousands of extra deaths from poor air quality." At the risk of being obvious, it takes a certain level of cruelty or indifference to call yourself pro-life when it comes to fetuses but not to breathing adults.

Democrats need to flip the script this year to help voters understand that federal regulation can save lives, jobs, and money. The core insight is that federal civil servants are not some "Deep State" cabal but public health experts who make decisions after congressional enactment, public proceedings, and court review. The issue isn't whether to regulate some product or service but *who* should—private companies or elected officials? Should the president of Dow Chemical decide what's a cancer-causing agent in the workplace or the presidentially appointed administrator at OSHA?

Yet Democrats have largely punted in the rhetorical contest over "big government." So, they now need to walk voters and the media through these paces:

Step 1 is to understand that evaluating regulations based merely on cost-benefit tests can be as neutral as literacy tests in the Old South. For (a) they're often based on self-serving companies exaggerating the costs and underplaying the benefits of proposed rules, and (b) you can't measure the value of, for one example, a Grand Canyon without smog.

Step 2 is to explain that regulation does *not* automatically kill jobs and add costs. Whatever effect Clean Air Act standards had on 55,000 remaining coal jobs nationally (one-third the number that work for McDonald's alone), it's dwarfed by the eight million jobs connected to the clean energy sector, according to the Department of Energy. Regulatory law enforcement also can force company engineers to create breakthrough technologies, which is how gas mileage on new cars has kept improving.

Step 3 is to realize that prevention is preferable to compensation—who wouldn't choose to keep their arms rather than be compensated for losing them in an industrial accident?

Step 4 is to explain that the alternative to regulation was described in the title of an enormously popular documentary in the 1930s—*100,000 Guinea Pigs*. Free market economists can sound authoritative when they calmly explain that the "perfect market," to use a phrase of economists, will send signals about

what to not purchase based on complaints about defective products. Worked great with thalidomide and the Corvair.*

That is, what Republicans and big business don't want to
talk about is the cost of *not* regulating. Take two recent examples in comparable economies.

In June, 2019, a small fire in one kitchen of a London
residential building called Grenfell Tower soon engulfed
all twenty-seven floors due to polyethylene material on the
exterior of the structure that lit it up like a match; in one
of the worst fires in modern UK history, seventy-six residents died due to a failure to regulate building construction. Canada cut back significantly in its fire prevention
and enforcement efforts, which allowed hundreds of wildfires to spread uncontained in the summer of 2023, as a
reddish haze of unhealthy smoke from them settled over
Northeastern cities.

Consequently, freedom of speech allowed Ohio Senator
J. D. Vance to get on his soapbox to rail against costly regulation . . . at the same time, freedom from harm politically
inspired him to rush to the small white town of East Palestine,
Ohio after a dangerous multicar train derailment in 2022.
There he sounded like some Norma Rae complaining about
inadequate federal train regulation under Biden (except it had

---

* This section draws on two books written by or sponsored by the author: respec-
tively, *Business Law on the War* (1979) and *Freedom from Harm: The Civilizing
Influence of Health, Safety and Environmental Regulation* (1986, written by David
Bollier and Joan Claybrook). Also, for a sharp look at how civil servants—
"bureaucrats" in political conversation—advance health and safety, see Michael
Lewis's *The Fifth Risk: Undoing Democracy* (2019).

been Trump who opposed stricter new laws for train safety). Heads they win, tails you lose.

So, when a neighbor or rival only blabs about the cost side of the regulatory ledger, Democrats need to bluntly call them out: "Why should parents support candidates who worry more about the profits of big corporations rather than the health and safety of their families? Why are you soft on corporate crime?" The GOP will prevail if the debate stays at the level of abstract slogans, but Democrats can win when regulations are explained both as law enforcement efforts and in vivid life-and-death terms.

FREEDOM OF RELIGION: *On a Right Wing and a Prayer*

When President Franklin Delano Roosevelt in 1941 declared the importance of religious freedom in his now-famous "Four Freedoms Speech," it wasn't a hard call. After fleeing religious persecution in Europe, arriving settlers in the seventeenth century were intent on securing their freedom to worship without state interference. By the late eighteenth century, the US Constitution twice established what Jefferson later called "a Wall of Separation between Church and State" no religious test for public office and, according to the very first words of the Bill of Rights, "Congress shall make no law respecting an establishment of religion, or prohibiting the free exercise thereof." Here's what James Madison—the "Father of the Constitution"—wrote in 1803: "The purpose of separation of church and state is to keep forever from these shores the ceaseless strife that has soaked the soil of Europe in blood for centuries."

Whatever jurists mean by "settled law," this would seem to be an example. But Jefferson, Madison, and Roosevelt did not anticipate Mike Johnson, who in 2023 became the highest-ranking Christian nationalist ever to serve in the American government, the result of a comedy of errors involving Speaker Kevin McCarthy and Rep. Matt Gaetz. Johnson seemed so intent on tearing down that "wall" that it was as if he put his hand on a copy of the Constitution while taking an oath to the Bible. "When I'm asked my world view, I simply say, 'well, go pick up a Bible.'"

Now the speaker and second in the presidential line of succession, Johnson—with the exception of Donald Trump—is probably the most dangerous MAGA man in the inflection election of 2024. He's a "friendly extremist"—he may look like an accountant, smile like a car salesman, and speak in the comfortable cadence of a radio talk show host, but his views reflect not the freedom to practice religion but his desire to impose it.

- "You can't even argue with a straight face that this did not begin as a Christian nation," he has confidently announced. Odd then that the US Constitution mentions God . . . never. Nor did the *Federalist Papers* explaining our founding document, nor did the Articles of Confederation that preceded both. Indeed, the original motto of the country, chosen by Adams, Jefferson, and Franklin, was "E Pluribus Unum"—"out of many,

---

† See two *Mother Jones* articles on Speaker Johnson and faith: Madison Pauly, "Mike Johnson's Long Flirtation with Christian Nationalism," https://bitly.ws /36gRc; David Corn. "Mike Johnson Hates America but Believes He Can Save It" http://bit.ly/41pZteZ.

one"—which was seen as a homage to pluralism, not
religion.

- He has called America "depraved . . . a completely
amoral society," sought to criminalize gay sex, called
homosexuality "bestial . . . unnatural," and worried that
it "could lead to people marrying their pets"—and, with
his wife, conducted seminars in churches that included
the injunction "Keep God in government."
- He wants a national abortion ban, with criminal
penalties for the women who get them and doctors who
perform them.
- He's among a group of Fox hosts and fundamentalists
who worry about something they call the "War on
Xmas" (sure looks like Xmas is winning) and how
the country is systematically biased against itself—in
other words, anti-Christian. Based on such imagined
victimhood, his coreligionists would benefit from
studying how persecuted minorities actually suffer
from anti-Semitism, racism, Islamophobia, and
homophobia. Jennifer Rubin explains their anxiety in
The Washington Post:

> *Well, there is a straightforward . . . explanation
> for why this group feels besieged—they are losing
> ground. . . . Writes Robert P. Jones, president of
> the Public Religion Research Institute. "As recently
> as 2006, white evangelical Protestants comprised
> nearly one-quarter of Americans (23%). By the time
> of Trump's rise to power, their numbers had dipped to
> 16.8%. Today, white evangelical Protestants comprise
> only 13.6% of Americans."*

With those kinds of numbers, the responsible thing for any interested party would be to think about "fixing" what's wrong by adapting to a changing market. Instead, many in this cohort have doubled down, becoming foot soldiers in the red-hatted MAGA movement. The decline isn't going to be reversed by angry, gray-haired folks demanding abortion bans and "don't say gay" bills

Then there's the Speaker's odd view about not God's law so much as secular law: though a lawyer, he explained his delay in releasing thousands of hours of January 6 tapes from inside the Capitol because he had to blur the faces of the rioters since "we don't want them to be retaliated against and charged by the Department of Justice." That seems pretty close to an obstruction of justice, not to mention his personal participation with Trumpers around January 6 and his vote against certifying the electoral count that night. Unlike Iran, Saudi Arabia, and Spain during the Inquisition, America has a strong tradition that the government will neither advance nor repress religion. We instead put our faith in law, democracy, and freedom, no matter how far outside the mainstream the speaker of the House happens to be. (For the best recent book on religious political extremism, see Tim Alberta's *The Kingdom, The Power*

---

‡ Here's what Donald Trump, who never attends church, said about religion and his fall opponent, a devout Catholic who attends services every weekend: "Catholics, you cannot vote for the Democrats. You can't even think about voting for Biden" who would supposedly prosecute them for their faith. Imagine Biden being taken seriously if he asserted with a straight face that Trump is dedicated to doubling taxes on white billionaires who regularly golf.

and the Glory: American Evangelicals in an Age of Extremism. Said *New York Times* book reviewer Jennifer Szalai, "Under the veneer of Christian modesty simmers an explosive rage . . . to act as though their highest calling is to own the libs." Alberta's book explains how evangelicals are evolving from a religious to a secular faith due to their idolatry of Trump.)

ABORTION: *Compulsory Pregnancy or Bodily Freedom?*

Politics has come a long way since Nixon successfully campaigned against "acid, amnesty and abortion" in 1972. Now pot is legal in most states. Trumpers want amnesty for insurrectionists, and abortion may be the issue that politically rescues Democrats in 2024 (as it did in 2022 when it shrank expected GOP pickups).

A long essay in *Democracy Journal* by abortion-rights advocate Ilyse Hogue lays out the story well. The 1973 *Roe v. Wade* decision emerged from a long gestation starting with women getting the right to vote in 1921 through to the 1960s women's movement, the Civil Rights Movement, and the Pill. Because the Constitution doesn't talk about abortion one way or the other, the 7-2 majority—including four of five Republican-appointed justices—gave women bodily rights under a new privacy umbrella. Justices Alito, Gorsuch, Barrett, Thomas, and Roberts all fundamentally considered it settled law at their Senate confirmations years later.

Until they unsettled it on June 24, 2022. What changed was not the Constitution nor the facts, but the Court once Trump's three justices took their seats. "The inescapable conclusion is that a right to an abortion is not deeply rooted in the Nation's history and traditions," declared Justice Alito in the majority opinion in *Dobbs*. Why, however, is that even the test since it tautologically assumes that progress is inherently bad—witchcraft and slavery at one point were also "traditions" before people realized that they were essentially immoral violations of basic freedoms. Anyone want to go back to those "traditions"?

The majority then added that *"Roe* was egregiously wrong from the start" which inevitably raises the question—did they all lie at their confirmation hearings when they brushed aside any concerns about the decision? To give themselves some intellectual cover, Republican justices also concluded how democratic it would be to have voters in each state deciding whether to allow abortion nearly always, ban it, or something in between.

Their affection for democracy was rich since they didn't embrace that value in decisions involving the Voting Rights Act and gerrymandering. Indeed, as the majority knew well, red state gerrymandered legislatures would tilt against liberalizing abortion laws. "It's not the American constitutional order" however, argued Jeet Heer in the *New Republic,* "that issues of fundamental rights belong to the 'democratic process' rather than the courts. [That] logic could just as easily overturn Supreme Court cases affirming a constitutional right to birth control (affirmed in 1965's *Griswold* decision), to marry people of different races (1967's *Loving* decision), or to marry people of the same gender (2015's *Obergefell* decision)." On such fundamental issues, freedom and privacy should not vary with someone's zip code.

Indeed, if the true test is majority consent, the decision has proven very unpopular. In all seven statewide referenda on the subject in the past two years, the antiabortion side lost by about 60-40 percent, including in red states like Kansas and Ohio. A poll of registered voters conducted by Navigator Research in June 2023 found that 60 percent said they considered themselves pro-choice, while 33 percent opposed abortion rights. A majority of Democrats (79 percent) and independents (63 percent) said they considered themselves pro-choice, as did 37 percent of Republicans. Majorities of White, Black, Latino, and Asian voters also said abortion should remain legal in all or most cases.

Beyond logic and law, the personal and political impact soon became obvious. Though only 1 percent of all one million annual abortions occur after twenty-one weeks, according to the CDC, most red states enacted laws either banning them altogether or with narrow exceptions in the third trimester.

Cases emerged of women forced to carry nonviable fetuses for months because doctors declined to perform abortions fearing possible criminal prosecution under state laws. In Tennessee, thirty-two year-old Mayron Hollis received an emergency hysterectomy after "excessive bleeding" when doctors refused to end her pregnancy. She only survived due to a large transfusion of blood, but the surgery left her unable to bear more children. And in the highly publicized case of Kate Cox in Texas, her doctors said that her life and fertility were at risk but the Texas Supreme Court—with no judge being a medical expert—refused to permit an abortion, forcing her to flee the state to obtain one because of her deteriorating health. (When asked after *Dobbs* what he would do about women inseminated by rapists, Gov. Abbott blithely said that they'd "end rape." [Could that work with hurricanes and floods too?] Tragically, data from 2023 identified over 26,000 women in Texas with rape-related pregnancies.)

The fight over "freedom for whom?" when it comes to abortion may soon get worse. Mifipristone, a nonsurgical abortifacient, has been FDA-approved for twenty years and taken safely by five million American women—and in dozens of other countries—with few if any side effects. Yet the pro-life lobby engaged in radical "forum shopping" by bringing a case to reverse the FDA approval where only a far-right Trump District Court appointee would rule on it and then be reviewed by the archconservative Fifth Circuit Court of Appeals. Presto! Judge Matthew J. Kacsmaryk overruled the FDA deciding he knew better than agency testing and twenty years of actual experience with a drug with a .00005 percent rate of injury or death (Viagra being ten times worse). Fifth Circuit Judge James Ho actually concluded that Texas plaintiffs had standing to sue because they might suffer from "aesthetic injury" by being denied the "profound joy" they felt seeing the fetus in a sonogram. (That was probably the only time that "joy" and "standing" have been used together in the same paragraph.)

The case is pending in the Supreme Court. SCOTUS will, in the author's opinion, either delay its decision until after the '24 election by remanding the case to the lower court on some technicality or decide in favor of the FDA because, otherwise, abortion may cost Republicans another national election. Of course, on the other hand, Alito and Thomas et al. may not care about the electoral viability of the Republican Party.

But the trend-line is clear—a significant majority of adults want the freedom to choose. And when it comes to reproductive rights, they agree with Shirley Chisholm over the Heritage

Foundation. Chisholm, the first Black woman ever elected to Congress, framed it best back in 1969: "The question is not: can we justify abortions, but can we justify compulsory pregnancy? What is more immoral, granting an abortion or forcing a young girl . . . to assume the responsibilities of an adult while she is still a child?" Yet a half century later, the Heritage Foundation's *Project2025* anticipates an actual Republic of Gilead where the next Republican president would start a program of mass "abortion surveillance"—its phrase—through the CDC in order to help prosecute doctors, pill distributors, and women.

The party that forces pregnant people to travel across state lines to get abortions—risking arrest and imprisonment—will lose votes and elections. A massively unpopular ruling and restrictive laws cannot forever endure in a country renowned for its history of freedom and majority rule.

LGBTQ: *"SAY Gay" in Campaigns*

Perhaps the only thing less likely than Democrats one day suddenly denouncing MSNBC and Netflix is the party of Tucker Carlson and Ted Cruz lacking fresh ways to electorally frighten their traditional followers. "Commies, peaceniks, deficits" worked decades back but have apparently run out of steam.

Searching for a new Achilles' heel in the 2024 cycle to aim at, GOP strategists have apparently found a new one from an old scarecrow—gay Americans.

If the basis of intolerance is fear of the other, the "threat" of gays abusing children as a political weapon has variously risen or receded over time. Anita Bryant's homophobic "Save our Children" Christian crusade in the 1970s was perhaps its high point . . . but then declined as more people became alarmed that some gay family members or friends would suffer discrimination despite our founding belief in "equal justice for all." (FYI, Bryant's granddaughter is married to a woman.)

It's hard to think of a political movement that went more quickly from opprobrium to accomplishment than gay rights. It was a relatively brief forty-six years from the Stonewall Riots in 1969 to "don't ask, don't tell" for military personnel in 1993 and then to the 2015 Supreme Court decision in *Obergefell* providing constitutional protection to same-sex marriages.

But like *Jaws 3*, a less ominous version is back. The latest round kicked off when the Arkansas legislature in 2021 overrode a veto by Gov. Asa Hutchenson to ban transition medication or surgery. Smelling blood in the water, twenty states have since either adopted that anti-transition posture and/or expanded the new homophobia agenda to include bans on (a) books in public schools that suggested tolerance of LGBTQ people; (b) drag shows that children might see; and (c) high school and college trans athletes—all one hundred of them out of forty million kids ages twelve to twenty-two—who wanted to compete on teams not of their birth gender (mostly transgender girls in female events).

It gets worse. Republican political consultants made sure to get their clients to use buzzwords like "grooming"—sexualizing—young children by predatory teachers; another is "parental rights," which sounds innocent enough until you realize that one or two insistent parents out of an entire school could now dictate the curricula for all students. Overall, the Human Rights Campaign estimates that twenty-nine out of 315 anti–LGBTQ bills proposed in 2022 were enacted in states around the country.

Could this new crusade win votes? Recent polling shows that while two-thirds of Americans—including 49 percent of Republicans—were in favor of same-sex marriages (PPRI), 58 percent thought that transgender students should only compete on teams that matched the sex they were assigned at birth (Pew).

Politically, it's probably futile if not counterproductive for individual Democratic candidates to defensively provide detailed responses to any of scores of possible anti-LGBTQ proposals. It is better to rely on credible medical experts such as the American Academy of Pediatrics who conclude that transition care should be available to minors; the Biden administration is now working through a federal rule that tries to thread the needle on transgender people in sports; a cavalry of corporations and celebrities, who earlier successfully stalled fights over bathrooms, will likely arise to denounce the new Anita Bryant wannabes (can't wait for Taylor Swift—actually—to weigh in here with her 270 million followers across several social platforms); and courts that'll be overturning such laws as violations of constitutional norms.

But two affirmative tactics are within the control of a progressive candidate: hit back in debates and interviews with (a) the importance of the "Equality Act" (H.R. 5) that would prohibit discrimination based on sexual orientation in employment, housing, credit, education, and public accommodations; and (b) meta-narratives about freedom in America when the pitchforks of homophobia come out. Say:

Why do Republicans hate gay people? Gay-bashing is not an American value. It's shameful that my opponent refuses to believe in "equal justice under law . . . for all." Isn't he/ she ashamed that Canada has issued a travel advisory warning its gay citizens to avoid states with new laws that target them? Do you support H.R.5 that would assure that anyone in your family who came out as gay wouldn't be subject to discrimination? Where's your humanity?

* * *

So long as there are people who talk about freedom while practicing fascism, this tension will continue. As for the political contest about which party has a better claim on this venerable value and word, the Republican Right grabbed a head start by talking more often about freedom on stages with more flags. The 2024 election, however, may shift its meaning for open-minded people. Since Trump's North Star is obviously his own id and Johnson's is God, Democrats have an opportunity to end up as the party of freedom by the time we inaugurate the next president.

---

§ Political communications consultant Anat Shenker-Osorio, who advises numerous leading Democrats, tees it up: "A message is like a baton that needs to be passed from person to person to person . . . The first rule of messaging is: say what you're for, say what you're for, say what you're for, *then* explain how Donald Trump wants to take away long-assumed freedoms. [Such as:] 'Which side are you on? Americans who believe in liberty and justice for all? Or traitors inciting violence against our country and trying to take away our freedoms? This November, it's time to show which side you're on. Vote for Democrats.'"

INSERT I
TRUMP FOR DUMMIES: *All You Need to Know in His Own Words*

- ***Donald Trump,*** asked by CBS's Leslie Stahl why he keeps repeating the phrase "Fake Media," responded: "I do it to discredit you all and demean you all so when you write negative stories about me no one will believe you."
- ***Donald Trump*** told a top DOJ official to announce it was investigating extensive fraud in the 2020 election. "Just *say* it was corrupt and leave the rest to me."
- ***Donald Trump*** said after one 2016 primary, "I love the poorly educated."
- ***Donald Trump,*** asked by Laura Ingraham about his $450 million fine in the NY fraud case, replied, "It was a form of Navalny," comparing himself to the man his pal Putin had murdered.
- ***Donald Trump*** told Mike Pence when the latter said he lacked the authority to deny certification of 45's electoral loss: "You're too honest."
- ***Donald Trump*** told his communication director Stephanie Grisham in 2020, "It doesn't matter what you say so long as you repeat it."
- ***Donald Trump:*** "If you come after me, I'm coming after you."

- ***Donald Trump***: "If I happen to be president and I see somebody who's doing well and beating me very badly, I say go down and indict them."
- ***Donald Trump:*** "I got rid of *Roe v. Wade.*"

CHAPTER 2
WITHER DEMOCRACY?

There's no easy way to stop a major party that's intent on destroying Democracy.
                          —**George Packer**, *The Atlantic*

Republicans want to make it harder to vote and easier to cheat.
                          —**Marc Elias**, Esq.

As long as [our Democracy] can still vote out incompetent leaders and expose systematic lying and censorship, that's the single most important competitive advantage a country can have.
—**Tom Friedman**, *New York Times* columnist

Mitch McConnell is many things but a fool is not one of them. When he told his caucus a decade ago that there were only two red lines they could not cross—laws to make voting easier and raising big corporate campaign contributions harder—he was simply reflecting reality. In a country where the GOP has now won the popular vote for president just once in the past thirty-five years, he had a choice between rigging elections or losing them. So a confederacy of cheaters it would be.

Of course, the GOP indignantly rejects that formulation. But Michigan State Representative John Pappageorge was caught acknowledging in 2004: "If we do not suppress the Detroit vote, we're going to have a tough time in this election cycle." A cocky Rudy Giuliani bragged to Steve Bannon on the latter's podcast that his 1993 mayoral campaign falsely advertised to Latinos that immigration agents were checking documents at the polls. The indicted and impeached attorney general of Texas, Ken Paxton, publicly claimed that he threw out 2.5 million mail-in ballots in 2016 from the very Democratic Harris County "or Trump would not have won the state." RNC advisor Clet Mitchell is now traveling around the country urging state parties to oppose locating voting places near liberal university campuses. Ex-senator Rick Santorum, trying to explain the success of Ohio's pro-abortion referendum in November 2023, said, "Thank goodness that most of the states don't allow you to put everything on the ballot because pure democracy is no way to run a country."

Indeed, claims about "voter fraud" have proven as reliable as aliens being secretly held in Roswell, New Mexico. All reputable investigations turned up next to nothing—as William Barr, Mark Meadows, and the Trump campaign's own internal campaign audits confirmed.

Now that McConnell has admitted the obvious while election-liars keep brazenly pointing fingers at Democrats, the party of John R. Lewis has no political choice but to expose GOP manipulation and dishonesty: STOP MAGA/SAVE DEMOCRACY . . . VOTERS-IN/MONEY-OUT . . . TAX

BILLIONAIRES TO HELP CHILDREN or some version should become a galvanizing issue since the franchise is the engine that drives democracy.

Yes, high food prices will be an issue this fall. But democracy is priceless.

* * *

Historically, "democracy"—"a government of, by, and for the people," in Lincoln's still classic formulation—has rarely made it onto the top ten concerns in national elections. Voters can personally understand and see, say, pump prices, crime data, and the pollution of a town's river . . . then vote accordingly. More people obviously wonder about sports scores or the Dow Jones Index rather than ask friends, "Hey, how's democracy doing?" As best-selling author and surgeon Atul Gawande wrote in the *New York Times,* "I've excised [cancerous] abdominal masses bigger than your head. . . . Someone blurts out, 'How could we let that thing get so huge?' Even the patients are mystified. One day they looked in the mirror and the mass seemed to have ballooned overnight. It hadn't of course. Usually it's been growing for years."

The cancer on democracy began growing at America's birth. Of course, the Constitution didn't allow women or Black people to vote and created an electoral college at the insistence of slave states that didn't want to lose their "heritage" of free labor. The 1798 Alien and Sedition Act, *Dred Scott,* the Civil War, the Ku Klux Klan, the Palmer Raids in the 1920s, American fascism in the 1940s, McCarthyism in the 1950s, Jim Crow laws in the 1960s, Watergate, and *Buckley v. Valeo* and *Citizens United v.*

FEC (the Supreme Court decisions that supercharged money in elections): all were anti-majoritarian assaults that took decades of struggle to counter. With mixed results:

- Millions of Black citizens can't vote because of state laws that deny the franchise to felons (even in non-capital cases);
- States with Republican governors and supermajority legislatures on party-line votes draw gerrymandered district lines that enable 99 percent of incumbents to win and 50 percent of voters to choose 75 percent of elected officials;
- Gerrymandered districts have reduced the number of authentically competitive House swing districts from fifty a decade ago to perhaps only twenty-five now;
- Thousands of talented but unwealthy citizens can't get out of the electoral starting blocks against multimillionaire opponents;
- In many of the most important contests, very well-funded outside special-interest groups outspend the candidates themselves;
- Voter roll purges in red states suspiciously knock off far more Democrats than Republicans, like when 90 percent of names struck in Florida in 2018 were Democrats before DeSantis won his gubernatorial contest by .4 percent; and
- People can nearly instantaneously get a facsimile of a check they wrote two years ago from their bank yet

may have to wait four, six, or eight hours on a line to vote.

It's not hard to understand why "The Democracy Index" published annually by *The Economist*—which analyzes countries based on their electoral process, political participation, civil liberties, and political culture—calls the United States a "Flawed Democracy" and ranks it only twenty-sixth in the world, behind Chile but just ahead of Estonia. A separate grading by Freedom House saw a sharp decline in the vitality of democracy in the United States over the past decade, as we fell measurably below the United Kingdom and Germany.

Those scores could shrink further. For now come two men—Donald Trump and Mike Johnson—who would have been laughed off the national stage as fringy Birchers in the 1950s yet seek to govern us based on their foundational beliefs; respectively, the *Forbes* 400 in Trump's case and the literal Bible for Johnson. President Biden called Trumpism "the most serious threat to democracy since the Civil War" in July 2022, well before Trump basically corroborated that conclusion with his "vermin" speech in November 2023 and promise to run a campaign of "revenge and retribution." And his involvement with the Heritage Foundation's *Project2025*, 889 pages of the most far-right ideas in American history, lays down their specific steps to American-style Orbán-ism.

What then are the feasible "checks and balances" in our governing system that can now slow or stop their plans? One is obvious but so far hopeless—when it comes to authoritarianism, Trump's Republican Party cowers before "General Zod." Tough talk from then Speaker Kevin McCarthy and Majority

Leader Mitch McConnell led to zero action after January 6 and a second impeachment that fell only ten GOP votes short of conviction.

There are at least five other guardrails to stop our careening democracy, with varying plausibility:

1. The '24 Election

The ideal solution would be for Democrats to make "extremism isn't patriotism" and "book bans are anti-American" winning issues this fall—from the president on down. And for them to use language and messages that not only persuade the head but also quicken the heart, passion being no less politically persuasive than reason. Biden indeed does deliver stirring speeches warning how the MAGA fraction of America wants to impose its red state fanaticism. To turn on and turn out low-propensity voters, he and allies need to more broadly craft a New Patriotism (see concluding chapter) that would deny the GOP its luster as the party of 1776; move beyond defense spending as the measure of Americanism; advance the positive values of freedom and rights; and unrelentingly condemn the Far-Right for blocking minimum wage increases, tax hikes on billionaires, cleaner air, safer guns, reproductive rights, racial justice, student loan relief, and universal voter registration. All enjoy large majority support.

Or as Bill Clinton put it, "you can't love your country and hate Democracy."

2. The Courts

Chapter 4 describes in detail how our independent judiciary has so far largely risen to the occasion, once an apparently overwhelmed Attorney General Merrick Garland finally stepped aside when it came to prosecuting Trump's alleged crimes. With many months of verdicts and appeals to go, there's now an avalanche of confessions and evidence that expose Trump and his accomplices as a de facto criminal syndicate. And private litigation in defamation lawsuits—by the Dominion Voting Systems against Fox News, E. Jean Carroll against Trump, and two election workers against Giuliani—led to huge payouts to the plaintiffs.

Trump is now implying that the entire judicial system is somehow all colluding against him, a conspiracy theory so vast that no sentient person could believe it. . . . though small dollar donors apparently do. GOP politicians will say it to keep their voters agitated and distracted but they cannot rationally *believe* it. For now, Trump is prosecuting his case in two jurisdictions: he is tied in a political presidential contest where he can successfully threaten to unleash his violence-prone base on party members; however, he is something like one for eighty in court cases, which are decided not by intimidation but by the rules of law and evidence. Which will come first, a political verdict in November or a legal one before then?

No wonder he spent $52 million on lawyers in 2023 since he's far weaker on trial than on the trail.

3. Voting Laws

There's an infinite number of ways for malicious partisans to cheat in elections by disenfranchising opponents, all without the need to admit what they're doing: reduce the number of specially designed "drop boxes" for mail-in ballots in minority areas; prohibit Sunday voting so that Black congregants can't easily go "from pews to polls"; slash voter rolls because of contrived "voter fraud" claims; refuse or strictly limit early voting or the distribution of mail-in ballots via the postal service; or require the production of "Voter ID" to qualify to vote.*

Previously, it took years of legislation and litigation to ban "literacy tests," which had been used to frustrate younger and minority voters. That led to the monumental Voting Rights Act of 1965 which, among other things, allowed the Department of Justice to "pre-clear" proposed voter restrictions by states with a history of them. The impact was jarring: while pre-Act there had been 280 Black local and state officials around the country, by 2006 that number had risen to 9,500.

Apparently that was too many, according to the 5-4 *Shelby County v. Holder* decision of 2013, when Chief Justice John Roberts figured out how to strike down a twice-renewed law (once by a unanimous Senate, including Strom Thurmond). His majority opinion basically boiled down to his comment at oral argument that the South had changed, like Trump's ex cathedra prediction after just fifteen deaths that COVID would soon "disappear." (He was merely a million-plus American deaths off.)

According to a Brennan Center analysis of mid-2023, the Roberts' rationale was similarly discredited when most of the Southern states he had lauded for being post-racial immediately

---

* Voter ID has discouraged some young and elderly Black voters though it does poll favorably due to the facile analogy of air travelers being required to show an ID before boarding a plane. But (a) air travel is not a constitutionally protected right like voting and (b) while a fake vote is bad, a fake ID plus a suicide vest on a plane is very, very bad. And simply signing the ballot on penalty of criminal prosecution seems nearly ironclad as compared to suppressing the vote.

started passing new anti-franchise laws. Texas did so on the day of the decision; since then, one hundred voter suppression state laws have been enacted. After the January 6 Insurrection, thousands of death threats poured into the offices of local election officials, frightening many into retirement; at the same time, political vigilantes, some in tactical gear, patrolled and filmed voters outside ballot drop boxes to supposedly hunt for nonexistent "fraud."

In this version of trench warfare, Republicans are well-positioned and highly motivated. There are nineteen states with election deniers among its top election officials. "If the Democrats pass the Voting Rights bill," argues a frightened Rep. Matt Gaetz, "Republicans will never win another election ever again."

Marc Elias's Democracy Docket is now in court in forty cases to block such proposed laws. Already, federal judges have found that Republicans in Alabama, Louisiana, Georgia, South Carolina, Wisconsin, and Florida used their redistricting power to discriminate against Black voters after the 2020 census. A federal district judge overturned Florida's SB 2050, which attempted to make it illegal for unqualified voters even to volunteer in voter registration drives. Unfortunately, such challenges may be ultimately decided by nine umpires who, as Roberts memorably but misleadingly put it at his confirmation hearing, merely call "balls and strikes."

4. The Extreme Court

The problem with that general metaphor is that those assigned to defend our constitutional democracy might end up overturning it. Today's SCOTUS eerily mirrors America in 1938, when a far-right, unpopular Supreme Court kept reversing the popular anti-Depression program of a Democratic president.

Roosevelt's very controversial response was to propose adding four more progressive justices to better align public sentiment and public law. But the pejorative phrase "court-packing" stuck and sunk the idea in Congress. Except . . . FDR's gambit ricocheted to pressure some of the hidebound jurists to unexpectedly resign or alter their opinions.

The judiciary was supposedly the "least dangerous branch," in the famous phrase of Alexander Hamilton. But that was before today's 6-3 "supermajority" of reactionary justices showed that is also way out of step with the needs and views of Americans. For although presidencies since 1978 have been evenly split between the two major parties, two-thirds of the justices have been chosen by only one party—including two Republican presidents who lost the popular vote yet went on to nominate five of the current six in the majority. And only Republicans have been chief justices over the past fifty-four years—nearly a quarter of our country's existence.

How did this happen? Bad luck and bad actors.

- Senate judiciary chairman Joe Biden in 1991 wouldn't extend Clarence Thomas's confirmation hearings another day or two to allow waiting witnesses to confirm Anita Hill's accusations of sexual misconduct.

---

† For excellent books on today's Court, see Michael Waldman's *The Super-Majority*, Steve Vladeck's *Shadow Docket*, and Joan Biskupic's *Nine Black Robes*.

- Justice Sandra Day-O'Connor resigned in 2005 to take care of her husband with Alzheimer's, to be replaced by committed Republican partisan Samuel Alito.
- After the death of Justice Scalia in 2016, Majority Leader Mitch McConnell violated all prior norms by refusing to even hold a confirmation hearing for Obama's nominee, moderate judge Merrick Garland.
- Then a lounge act became president in 2017 due to the 1789 electoral college and FBI Director James Comey needlessly reopening the criminal probe of nominee Hillary Clinton just days before Election Day. Donald Trump was therefore able to later, if barely, confirm Brett Kavanaugh to the vacant Scalia seat and then to easily appoint two more far-right justices, Neil Gorsuch and Amy Coney Barrett. (Carter served one term and had no Supreme Court nominations; Trump had three in his one term.)

If Hillary Clinton, who won nearly three million more votes than Donald Trump, had become president in 2017, today the Court lineup would be completely reversed to 6-3 in favor of Democratic-appointed justices. "If" is rarely a strong argument. But the sequence of appointments described has in fact produced among the most far-right and unpopular Courts in history, at odds with FDR legatee Joe Biden in a country increasingly multiracial and Democratic. The GOP acts as if it can party like it's 1938 again.

Today's SCOTUS has ironically turned into just the kind of activist court that conservatives have been complaining about for decades—except its activism seeks to overturn liberal precedents by finding any available technical basis or simply replacing stare decisis with new made-up precedent. Here's how the fix is in:

- *Abortion*: As previously discussed on pages 33–37, no decision of this Trump Court has proven as unpopular and influential as *Dobbs v. Jackson Women's Health Organization.* There's probably no better example of the cliché "be careful what you wish for" than making sure that people with uteruses are reminded at least once a month how they should vote.
- *Democracy:* As a young White House aide in 1973, John Roberts wrote a memo on why Nixon should challenge the 1965 Voting Rights Act as unconstitutional. That didn't happen. But two decades later, the same John Roberts, now the Chief Justice, got his wish by overturning Section 5 of the Act as unnecessary.

Roberts also was key to developing the rationale that money-is-speech in the *Citizens United* decision that allowed dark corporate money to swamp campaigns. And he wrote the 5-4 opinion in *Rucho v. Common Cause* in 2019 to allow even radical gerrymandering, such as when Wisconsin state candidates received 45 percent of the vote in local elections in 2020 yet controlled 64 percent of state legislative seats. That was obviously on its face a perversion of majority rule but also a "political question," wrote Roberts, who added that it was just too mathematically difficult to be resolved by an enforceable formula. (The decision was pre-ChatGPT and newer versions of artificial intelligence

[AI], which might soon solve the Chief Justice's supposed math problem.)

With the possible exceptions of Trump and Mitch McConnell, no one person has done more to damage democracy in America than John Roberts.

- *Religion*: Justice Thomas wrote the opinion that carved out an exception to the civil rights laws for bakers who said they didn't want to accommodate a gay couple. But since the baker was merely offering a service for hire on its website, it was a stretch for the Court to act as if they were exercising "speech". Justice Sonia Sotomayor dissented: "The Court for the first time in its history granted a business open to the public a constitutional right to refuse to serve members of a protected class."
- *Second Amendment*: The Court in 2007 overturned two hundred years of very settled law when Justice Thomas wrote that any future restriction had to demonstrate that the law had "deep historical roots." Which in turn led today's SCOTUS to actually question the constitutionality of a law barring men with restraining orders from having a right to a gun since there was no such law in 1791 . . . perhaps because domestic violence wasn't then a thing or a law.

  When Justice Scalia was asked why he didn't sign on to Thomas's opinion, he commented, "I'm an originalist, not a nut."
- *Race*: The Court overturned three decades of affirmative action precedent based essentially on this sneaky tautology from the Roberts majority opinion,

"The way to stop discrimination on the basis of race is to stop discriminating on the basis of race." Roberts tries to confuse discrimination and restitution by pretending that centuries of bias *against* people of color were as constitutionally suspect as trying to *help* that same victimized class. Charles Blow, a *New York Times* columnist and author of the best-selling memoir *Fire Shut Up in My Bones,* could hardly contain himself: "Reading that line was like having someone spit in my face. The Court takes the absurd position that racism must be ignored for racism to be overcome."

- *Ethics*: In 1969, it was reported that Justice Abe Fortas was being paid $20,000 a year by financier Louis Wolfson to teach a law school course and covertly advise him on legal troubles. (Wolfson eventually went to jail for Securities and Exchange Commission violations.) After continuing bad publicity, Fortas chose to resign. This contretemps should have reminded everyone that there had been a code of ethics for all federal judges, but not those at the top of this branch of government.

That was the worst ethical failure in SCOTUS history . . . until the independent media platform *ProPublica* exposed Clarence and Ginni Thomas in a multiheaded scandal far worse than what led to Fortas's resignation. After complaining five years ago to some allies that he might have to resign due to the Court's fixed salary, his in-kind income magically ballooned. Many secret plush trips were provided to the Thomases—courtesy of billionaires Harlan Crow and the Koch Brothers—each of whom had an interest in major cases affecting their wealth; at the same time, Federalist Society guru Leonard Leo was putting together a $150 million PAC to lobby for the confirmation of Court nominations and made a half-million dollar "gift" to Ginni's conservative group, Liberty Central, which then paid her a salary of $120,000, money that also went into the pockets of her husband on their joint checking account.

There's more. Crow—who owns one of the largest collections of Nazi memorabilia in the country—financed schooling for a boy Thomas was raising and purchased the home of the Justice's mother while she was living there. *And* loaned the couple $275,000—later forgiven—to purchase a first-class recreational vehicle camper that they used in the summer months when they weren't being feted in fancier digs.

Have I mentioned that Ginni, a well-known right-wing speaker and organizer, also personally contacted dozens of Republican state legislators to vote to overturn the 2020 election? "You can realize right now," she wrote Trump chief of staff Mark Meadow in the context of fake voter claims, "that there are no rules in war." A Justice who refuses to recuse in cases involving his seditionist spouse is quite the unicorn.

Senate judiciary chair Dick Durbin, a cautious institutionalist wary of looking partisan, had seen enough. He finally announced in late 2023 that his Committee would issue subpoenas and hold hearings into Thomas and Leo in order to consider an Ethics Code for the justices. "By accepting these lavish, undisclosed gifts, the justices have enabled their wealthy benefactors and others with business before the Court to gain private access to the justices. The highest court should not have the lowest ethics. . . . As long as the [Chief Justice] refuses to act, the Judiciary Committee will."

A petulant Justice Alito publicly insisted that "No provision in the Constitution gives [Congress] the authority to regulate the Supreme Court—period." But Justice Elena Kagan, former Dean at Harvard Law School, in effect replaced Alito's smug "period" with a comma to keep the conversation going: "It just can't be that the Court is the only institution that somehow is not subject to checks and balances from anybody else. We're not imperial. Can Congress do various things to regulate the Supreme Court? I think the answer is: yes."

The next month the Court slightly responded to the outside pressure and, with all justices in agreement, announced an Ethics Code in a defensive statement that lacked specificity or enforceability. They implied that they *had* been voluntarily complying with a version of an ethics code but, added Thomas disingenuously, he just didn't know that he was supposed to be reporting such in-kind gifts. Comedian-commentator Leslie Jones on *The Daily Show* wasn't buying it. "Having good judgment is the entire point of being a *judge!*"

It's impossible to take seriously the complaints of a party that previously held eight House show trials into Clinton-Benghazi while she was seeking the presidency and previously had run against the "Liberal Warren Court" for decades. So how can it be unkosher to now run against the "Corrupt Trump Court"? A position with constitutional lifetime tenure especially shouldn't confer lifetime immunity from fact-based public comment and inquiry.

5. "The Media"

It was among Jefferson's most celebrated observations: "Were it left to me to decide whether we should have a government without newspapers or newspapers without a government, I should not hesitate a moment to prefer the latter." Which is roughly why it's called "The Fourth Estate."

Yet like complaining about the weather, everyone complains how the media is mistreating them. Of course, however, there's no one "THE Media"—there are thousands of small to huge entities that spread the news (not even counting millions of Americans who have social media sites, any one of whom can make or spread news). Assessing its overall impact on democracy in one sweeping conclusion, for good or ill, is a fool's errand. But there's also no doubt that the fourth estate has a big say and sway on how voters think—spending by candidates on TV ads certainly makes it appear that they agree.

The "free media," on the one hand, can expose public corruption when lawmakers become lawbreakers—Watergate being the prime example. None have done it better than the *New York Times* and *Washington Post* defrocking Donald Trump as an incorrigibly corrupt liar, which no doubt contributed to the creation of the House Select Committee on January 6 and then subsequent criminal probes of Team Trump. But the media can also report conspiracy theories to inflame people—such as "Remember the *Maine*" in 1898, the Red Scare in the 1950s, and every night now on Fox "News." These very disparate performances lead to two clashing schools of thought when it comes to the interplay of media and politics.

First, in what can be called "both sides" journalism, reporters try to present both or all sides of a controversy in news articles so people can make informed decisions—the goal being "balance." That's been the accepted template for generations of journalists and editors . . . at least until Trump and MAGA came along to become falsehood factories under the cover of both-sides-ism. Amazingly, for nearly a decade now, the mainstream media has never successfully figured out how to respond to the willful, strategic lies by Team Trump other than by breathlessly repeating them.

Second, a newer template—best advanced by New York University's Jay Rosen, *The Atlantic*'s James Fallows, and media expert and author Brian Stelter—focuses more on truth than balance. In the words of ABC's George Stephanopoulos, after he five times asked #2 House Republican Steve Scalise in December 2023 if "Biden was legitimately elected" and five times couldn't get a yes-or-no answer: "We are a democracy that is decided by elections. If that's called into question, then our whole democracy can be called into question."

It may well be easier to just publish obvious lies by invoking the First Amendment (which applies to public government, not private companies) than to make difficult case-by-case judgments about each willful falsehood. But in a public contest between democracy and fascism, it would be strange if a Fourth Estate that exists due to constitutional protections didn't take a side against a top-down ideology that would muscle the media to being an arm of the state. Indeed, the upside of the Rosen/ Fallows/Stelter framework is pretty great—reducing the misinformation and disinformation that threatens to sacrifice truth on the altar of "fairness."

Admittedly, both parties play blame-the-media for their scandals or unpopularity. Which is rarely the whole truth but can be "a" truth. Consider just four important examples of why a free media is essential, though perhaps not adequate insurance against authoritarianism:

- **CNN:** In 2022, David Zaslav, CEO of Warner Bros-Discovery, which owns CNN, had conversations with John Malone, the company's largest shareholder and a well-known conservative corporate titan. The two arrived at the strategy of repositioning CNN by attracting GOP on-air guests and viewer eyeballs. First to go was Stelter, probably the leading national analyst of the media, for being unacceptably effective at disemboweling the Right Wing.

  As part of that process, Zaslav persuaded Trump to leave his safe harbor of Fox to do a CNN Town Hall meeting, as Biden had done previously. "He's the front-runner," Zaslav explained, "He has to be on CNN. We're happy he's coming."

  Made sense . . . but only if you ignore the reality that it was Trump who he was talking about. What happened next was one of the biggest self-inflicted wounds in mainstream media history. In May 2023, Trump spoke in front of a stacked audience of only MAGA enthusiasts, who laughed at his jokes, cheered his insults, and made it nearly impossible for an earnest moderator, Kaitlin Collins, to ask fair questions and respond to answers. He played the audience as if it were one of his Nuremberg-like rallies.

  A. H. Stoddard of *RealClearPolitics* and a regular on TV talk shows was appalled: "His lies were coming so

fast that [it was] a tool for dominance. So if you tried
to correct him, you're just a fly on the windshield."
Christiane Amanpour, CNN's leading foreign policy
commentator, was plainly embarrassed: "Maybe we
should revert back to the newspaper editors and TV
chiefs of the 1950s who in the end refused to allow
McCarthyism onto their page. So maybe less is more.
Maybe live is not always right."

The upshot of this controversy was that CNN's
executive director was unceremoniously fired and
Zaslav learned the hard way that the media divide in
today's sharply polarized politics is no longer simply
Left/Right but Right/Wrong based on honest reporting.
(And so far, under new leadership, Mark Thompson,
previously at the *New York Times*, has returned CNN
to tough questioning of Republican guests by skilled
journalists like Jake Tapper and Collins.

- **FOX:** It was both amusing and pathetic that a study
of how well-informed different TV audiences were
concluded that people who watched only Fox "News"
were less informed than those who watched *no* TV.

That should not be a shocker given its years of
actual fake news—weaving right-wing tropes, hatred of
Muslims and the homeless, double standards portraying
Trump and Biden, and a late-night lineup from a
universe of those who cite "alternate facts" (Conway)
and "truth isn't truth" (Giuliani). All this and more have
been extensively reported by @Media Matters well
before Fox's defamation of Dominion Voting Systems led
to a $787 million payout by the cable channel.

"What happened to Dad?" is the opening line
of a documentary and book by Jen Senko—*The
Brainwashing of My Dad*—that illuminates the effect
that Fox has on large numbers of viewers and voters.
In 2019, Senko became alarmed by how her normally
personable father, who had voted for Kennedy,
would periodically snarl about the "femi-nazis and
communists" in politics. She eventually realized that,
on his long commutes by car to and from work, he was
listening to Rush Limbaugh and Fox hosts unfiltered
and unchecked. Dad had quite simply turned into not a
conservative but a fanatic. It's said that those who don't
know who is the "mark" (sucker) in a game of poker
is usually him—for Fox, that would be most of their
viewers.

And no, MSNBC is not merely a liberal Fox. Its
hosts of course have strong points of view, but it is
unimaginable that any would appear on Democrats'
campaign stages or pull punches in interviews with
their preferred candidates. "By not fact-checking
false statements," observes Mara Gay of the *New York
Times* editorial board, "Fox is simply not engaged in
journalism but propaganda."

In rebuttal, owner Rupert Murdoch contended that
"most of the media is in cahoots with elites peddling
political narratives rather than pursuing the truth."
(Did he say "peddling political narratives"?) His heroic
self-image collided with the title of Ken Auletta's
definitive *New Yorker* profile on him—"The Pirate."
Later came the Dominion fiasco, where Fox star

anchors were exposed as political liars-for-hire when they said one thing about January 6 on air and another in simultaneous private email correspondence to their White House handlers. (In one precious email found during discovery, Tucker Carlson melted down after the channel accurately called the election for Biden: "Do the executives understand how much credibility and trust we've lost with our audience? We're playing with fire." This for reporting the news accurately.)

Fox is not only an IQ-killer but has also pioneered the much-discussed "Silo Effect" where tens of millions of viewers with a need to believe compel them to listen only to Fox. That infantilization of the audience completely undermines our notion of the vaunted "marketplace of ideas"—hence viewers learn far more about Hunter Biden's drug and sex life than about Joe Biden's strong economy. As the collective "mark," they cannot understand that, in fact, "news" about Hunter and Joe are not equal in importance.

But the formula works as intended. A study of ten thousand communities found that Fox persuaded between 3 and 28 percent of its viewers to vote Republican. Explains Oliver Darcy of CNN, "the mainstream media press has probably failed to match the energy necessary to effectively counter" the Big Lies repeated in Fox Land. Nixon's so-called "silent majority" has morphed into Trump's "loud minority."

- **MUSK:** It's getting harder to maintain the pretense of an informed electorate when so many libertarian oligarchs are calling the shots.

The latter media mogul, with a reported net
worth greater than seventy countries, cites the First
Amendment (again, which doesn't apply to his private
platform of X, formerly Twitter) to justify inviting
back white supremacists and neo-Nazis to his site
in a not-subtle effort to turn it into a digital Fox . . .
with the result so far of doubling the number of anti-
Semitic tweets while reducing by half the number
of X's followers and advertisers. It's one thing for a
major platform to carry obvious lies and slander but a
different level of poison when it's the owner himself who
amplifies hate like a reactionary racialist from South
Africa (which he is). Among scores of examples were
his skepticism about the physical assault on Paul Pelosi,
belief that "George Soros is an enemy of humanity,"
tone-deaf argument that appeals for "diversity"
are pure racism, and his buy-ins to the "The Great
Replacement Theory" and to the insanity that "Jews
hate white people."

No surprise then that anti-Semitism rose over
50 percent on Twitter shortly after Musk bought it
because, he said, of his devotion to "free speech."
(Until then, no First Amendment scholars had
considered an increase in anti-Semitism as evidence of
free speech.)

It's impossible to distinguish his views from those of
Tucker Carlson, whom he hired after Fox dumped him.
In the evolving contest between democracy and fascism,
Musk—at a level that includes only Trump, Johnson,
Murdoch, and Thomas—is a world-class exemplar

of extremism, evidence of the lethal combination of ignorance and arrogance. Nearly every tweet or retweet of his subtly or blatantly advances the Trump story line. He's apparently a helluva entrepreneur but his tweets reveal someone who thinks he's wise and witty yet has meager political sophistication.

- **THE *NEW YORK TIMES*:** It is the greatest newspaper in the world and, as mentioned, unsurpassed in exposing Trump's anti-Americanism. No one knows better how Trump thinks than Maggie Haberman, and no reporter keeps rebutting a big MAGA lie as often as Luke Broadwater humiliates James Comer's attempts to call repayment of a loan from father Biden to son Hunter as millions in Chinese cash. So, it's puzzling why there seems to be some invisible internal directive to bend over backward against saying that in headlines and article placement.

  For instance, after Trump first used Hitleresque language in November 2023, the paper initially ran this headline: "Trump Takes Veterans Day Speech in a Very Different Direction." That's one way to put Trump's open sprint to become an American dictator. Only after blowback to a later both-sides headline on the third anniversary of January 6 did the *Times* switch to a more accurate "3 Years after Jan. 6, Trump Clings to Campaign Message of Falsehoods." When (as discussed later) Trump killed a consensus bi-partisan border reform bill, their headline was "Crisis on the Border Dashes Biden's Hope of Reversing Policies," as if Biden had failed, instead of a more accurate one, "Trump,

Speaker Kill Reform to Keep Border a Hot Issue in '24." And after a Republican Special Counsel exonerated Biden in his confidential documents case, the Times ran far more pieces on gratuitous comments about Biden's age and far more than Trump's treasonous message to Putin that he could attack NATO. Is this ideological paranoia or a bend-over-backwardism to avoid the Gray Lady being called "liberal"?

Consider this hypothetical: a reporter bursts into any typical newsroom saying, "Can you believe this—the president just called a female senator a 'stupid bitch!'" Would that be big news? Yes if it were Biden, no if it were Trump. Right? But why? Since when has frequency of indecency become a defense?

* * *

Adding up all the media, we wouldn't have a semblance of a democracy without its protected information function. Yet much of it fails to share the whole truth about how radical and unprecedented Trumpism is due to its embrace of not only false equivalents but also a kind of journalistic Gresham's Law where personal attacks and horse-race coverage are easier and more profitable. As Les Moonvez, then the powerful head of CBS, said during the 2016 presidential race about Trump's entertainment value, "the ride we're all having now may not be good for America but it's great for CBS." Given how easily Trump could manipulate the mainstream media into repeating his lies and how ill-informed voters were about the economy through at least 2023, a significant reappraisal of the political media is overdue in 2025 based on George Packer's core observation in *The Atlantic*, "The for-profit model of journalism shows signs of being broken."

A century after commercial advertising saved print journalism, the advent of online reporting and advertising is drastically shrinking traditional media revenues and jobs, especially at local papers. Then there's a loss of trust in the Fourth Estate due in significant part to Trump's repeated disparagement of "the enemy of the people"—and distrusted media cannot play its role in holding power accountable. Is there nothing to be done as a kind of Gresham's Law of journalism encourages baseless personal attacks and mindless horse-race coverage to crowd out more substantive reporting? Do we simply watch capitalism devour democracy due to the deep pockets of reactionary billionaires as Musk, Murdoch, Malone, and Sinclair Broadcasting buy up independent media?

Starting the conversation were two California media watchers—Stephen Waldman and Jeff Jarvis. In his thoughtful analysis, for example, Waldman suggested the idea of content-free taxpayer subsidies to sustain journalists' jobs. The country subsidizes farming and doesn't tax churches because of the social value we put on each. What next then for the Fourth Estate? It's a big subject beyond the scope of this book.

CONCLUSION

Al Smith, the celebrated former governor of New York, once said that "all the ills of democracy can be cured by more democracy."

But that can't happen unless there's a rolling backlash starting in Fall 2024 that leads to a governing majority that can patriotically demand that our democracy be democratic. Then the following urgent fixes go from impossible to conceivable:

- First and foremost, candidates and members need to endorse the perfectly named "John R. Lewis Voting Rights Advancement Act" to end radical gerrymanders; enact universal registration based on Social Security files; and create a program of public money in public elections to help level the playing field and spotlight who's drowning us in "dark money." (One already successful component is a version of the New York City campaign finance law that matches donations under $175 at 6-1 for local voters.)
- Second, the Senate filibuster rule, which is a procedural standard enacted anew at the start of each Congress, allows twenty states with only 10 percent of the population to veto the other thirty states with 90 percent of our citizens. Filibusters delayed for decades an anti-lynching law and numerous civil rights acts. The Democratic Caucus in the 118th Congress got within a couple of senators of shutting it down when obstructionists Joe Manchin and Kyrsten Sinema voted "no," bragging that they were protecting minority rights (like an executioner protects the deceased from further disease).
- Third, the electoral college has proven to be an intergenerational ballistic missile against majority rule. One constitutional way to shoot that down without going the constitutional amendment route is the "National Popular Vote" (NPV). If enacted, states combining

for at least 270 electors agree to elect as president
the candidate who wins a plurality or majority of the
national popular vote. That number of states has now
reached a cumulative 205 electoral votes. If others with
Democratic governors and legislative majorities can now
sign on (Maryland [4], Michigan [15], Nevada [6]) and
then states that can add up to the final thirty-five do as
well (Arizona [11], New Hampshire [4], Pennsylvania [19],
Virginia [13], Wisconsin [10]), then the reign of the 1787
Connecticut Compromise that created the slave-state-
favoring electoral college is gone.

- Fourth, there would need to be at least two Supreme
Court vacancies in any second Biden term to break the
far-right hammerlock that the Federalist Society has on
the Roberts-Leo Court . . . which of course presumes a
"partisan" mortality time line and Democratic gains in
the House and Senate.

- Last, probably the greatest obstacle to a "strong
democracy" is the severe malapportionment of the
US Senate where twenty states with the combined
population of California have forty senators while
California has two. But presumably a constitutional
amendment to change that would never win over the
two-thirds supermajority of states required.

More plausible, however, is for Congress to enact legislation
that permits the addition or division of states to avoid a worsening geographical oligarchy in the Senate. This can be done
by adding states, as when the Dakotas in 1889 entered the
Union, with two states and four senators at the insistence of

the Republican Party. Puerto Rico and Washington, DC, for example, could become states . . . or some large blue state could theoretically be split into two.

For now this change is largely inconceivable, like the end of monarchy, slavery, and colonialism were at their peaks. The alternative though is also largely inconceivable—an America with a growing blue urban supermajority governed by low-population rural states. As Wyoming goes, so goes America?

That would not help our ranking in *the Democracy Index*.

CHAPTER 3
THE MAGA MOBOCRACY— America Held Hostage

Violence is as intrinsic to fascism as free speech is to democracy.
—Rick Stengel

I have the support of the police, the support of the military, the support of Bikers for Trump—I have the tough people, but they don't play it tough . . . unless they go to a certain point and then it would be very bad, very bad.
—President Donald Trump

I fear that the country is entering a phase of history with more organized domestic civil violence than we've seen in a hundred years.
—Philip Zelikow, executive director of the 9/11 Commission

Democracy is how people can live together and resolve their differences peacefully. There are two agreed-on ways to do that: free and fair elections and the rule of law. But should those two fail, there is a third option—the rule of law, when not arguments but arms settle scores. In its own category, of course, was the Civil War, which became an "irrepressible conflict" in which 700,000 Americans died once elections and courts could not resolve the untenable status quo of a country "half-slave and half free."

Violence can be exercised by state power—millions of indigenous people were relocated or killed to make way for white settlers; millions of Blacks were subdued by *Dred Scott,* the Black Codes, Separate-but-Equal, and Jim Crow. Or by private vigilantism—the 1863 Draft Riots in New York City, the Tulsa Race Massacre of 1921, the lynchings of 4,400 people of color over decades, and now largely young men with guns killing, on average, a hundred people a day.

Today, by their own admission, Trump and MAGAs will threaten, trigger, condone, or engage in violence when it's to their advantage. So they favor elections and laws so long as elections and laws favor them . . . but will ignore both if necessary to maintain power or fortune.

(It was almost comical that nearly all Republicans who agree with Trump that the 2020 election was marred by fraud don't consider their own victories on the same ballot to be tainted as well.) Trump's relentless insults of prosecutors and judges— like the scores of times he's called DOJ prosecutor Jack Smith "deranged" and a "thug"—created an air of violence that had the potential, if not intent, to intimidate witnesses and jurors. Two judges have had to issue partial gag orders because, in the words of Judge Tanya Chutkan, who is presiding over the January 6 case in Washington, D.C, "when defendant has publicly attacked individuals, including on matters relating to this case, those individuals are consequently threatened and harassed."

This is not conjecture. A Texas woman was charged with making death threats against her ("you are in our sights—we want to kill you") and, after a temporary suspension of a partial gag order in the New York Attorney General fraud case, the Jewish judge received serious threats that totaled, when transcribed, 275 single-spaced typewritten pages.

Sore losers is the nicest way to describe those who physically threaten members of the other party—anti-American fascists the more accurate since our social contract doesn't include a resort to violence for dispute resolution. The evidence is clear that this is not a "both-sides" problem:

- Mitt Romney disclosed a shocking secret to his biographer about his political tribe on exiting the Senate—some Republicans wouldn't vote to convict Trump of Articles of Impeachment because they personally feared violent retaliation against them and their families from the MAGA mob. Indeed, Romney attracted so many death threats that he paid $5,000 a day for extra security for himself and his family. Brendon Buck, who had been a top aide to Rep. Paul Ryan, Romney's VP pick, admitted that "the fear is real and pervasive—members fear for their lives and their safety. When you change your vote [on Impeachment], you might as well leave." Same thing with Andrew Hitt, the Wisconsin GOP chairman, who told *60 Minutes* he signed fake electors slate because he was afraid of being killed otherwise.

Other than the 1850s, has anything like this ever happened before or since in America?

- Over three-fourths of political violence comes from Far-Right domestic groups and individuals with the rest from foreign actors and the Left wing, according to federal crime data—and political violence is at its highest level since data was first collected in 1994.
- Red states have higher homicide rates and more school shootings and guns per capita—with the astonishing result that guns, to take one example, kill 490 times more Americans than guns kill the British as a percentage of their populations.
- Thirty-five percent of Republicans in polls say they're willing to use violence to obtain their political goals.
- Capitol Hill police reported that "the number of threats against Members of Congress rose three-fold from 3939 in 2017 to 9625 in 2021 as death threats also fill the in-boxes of teachers, local officials, and prosecutors seen as unfaithful to the MAGA catechism." A new category called "swatting" was invented to describe prank calls to law enforcement that a prosecutor or politician was being attacked in order to spur teams of police law to rush to the purported locations.
- In what seemed like a *Saturday Night Live* sketch, spokesman Steven Cheung denied any similarity between Trump and Hitler's remarks by blaming "Trump Derangement Syndrome . . . [and] their existence will be crushed when President Trump

returns to the White House." (To quote Molly Ivins, that probably sounded better in the original German.)

- What exactly was Trump intending to communicate by visiting a gun store in South Carolina in 2023 that happened to be the one that sold an AR-15 later used to carry out a racial mass slaughter? ("Of all the gun joints in all the towns in all the world. . .")
- Following a murder spree that took eighteen lives in Lewiston, Maine, in late 2023, a local law enforcement official was asked whether the shooter, Robert Card, had any accomplices. "Yes: Every goddamned Republican in the United States Congress—next question."
- And growing talk of a "new Civil War" now comes almost exclusively from the reactionary right— especially Lost Causists who apparently have not yet accepted either Appomattox in 1865 or the civil rights laws of the 1960s. Indeed, the term "mobocracy" gained purchase when Congressman Abraham Lincoln used it in the 1840s and '50s to describe people who tried to get their way through threats and violence, such as mobs that lynched prisoners.

"Knock the Crap Out of Them, Would Ya?": Menace as Strategy

Donald Trump, of course, didn't originate the strategy of implying or engaging in political violence—Brutus beat him to the punch by over two thousand years—but he is certainly now its leading proponent. Menace is not a bug but a feature of how he and his party—not Democrats—attempt to hold on to power and browbeat opposition.

Again, since the whole exceeds the sum of its parts, only an accumulation of examples can adequately convey how the vocabulary of violence is regularly and influentially deployed by Trump:

- Pre-presidency, Trump had a history of using violent language and imagery that meshed with his outsized displays of toxic masculinity, perhaps best embodied by his enthusiastic personal involvement with the theatrical brutality of WWE. His attraction included a significant financial investment in pro wrestling.
- A few months after the 1989 Tiananmen Square Massacre when the Chinese Communist government killed several thousand protesting students, Trump said that it was "vicious, horrible but they put it down with strength. That shows you the power of strength."
- At 2016 rallies, he'd regularly rouse crowds to scream obscenities at the assembled media and urged listeners once to "knock the crap out of them [protestors], would ya?" even promising to pay for lawyers if they were prosecuted (he never did).
- In the 2020 presidential debate with Biden, Trump was asked by moderator Chris Wallace to denounce violent supporters "like the Proud Boys." Trump replied, "I say, stand back and stand by" about a group whose leaders were later sentenced to terms of up to twenty-two years for their violent sedition on January 6.
- He chose the locations of Waco, Texas, and later Tulsa, Oklahoma—places whose very names arouse far-right militias—to give key campaign speeches. On the

anniversary of Juneteenth in Tulsa, he explained with no subtlety to his online audience, "please understand you will not be treated like you have been in New York, Seattle, or Minneapolis." In response, Kellen Browning, the head of Twitch, the live streaming platform, said it was suspending President Trump's channel for "hateful conduct," in what appeared to be the first deliberate suspension of one of Trump's social media accounts.

- His dark Inaugural Address in 2017 pivoted on a metaphor that unspecified "carnage" would no longer be tolerated. Yet as president, he would joke about it, drawing nervous laughter from an audience of police officers on Long Island by suggesting that they "not be too nice" when apprehending suspects.

- His penchant for appearing "tough" especially flared up before and during massive protests following the videotaped suffocation and murder of George Floyd by a white Minneapolis police officer on May 25, 2020. He then declared that "when they loot, we shoot." The night before scheduled protests in DC, Trump warned that those who got too close to the White House would confront a Secret Service "with the most vicious dogs and ominous weapons"—"vicious dogs" obviously evoking frightening images from the 1960s. According to Secretary of Defense Mark Esper's memoir *Sacred Duty*, Trump asked him, "You can't just shoot them, simply shoot them in the legs or something like that?" At a later meeting, he suggested to Gen. Mark Milley that troops "should crack their skulls."

- The next day, June 1, 2020, largely peaceful crowds were dispersed by tear gas canisters as low-flying helicopters dropped "bang" grenades. Trump then used this tumult as cover to march across Lafayette Park with a few dozen top law enforcement and military leaders to create a photo op holding up a Bible in front of historic St. John's Church where a fire had been set in a wastepaper basket. A disgusted Steve Schmidt said, "In ten minutes, he totally disgraced his office and committed a sacrilege." (Later Milley publicly apologized for his participation in uniform at the staged event.)

  Twenty-three former homeland and national security experts, including two Bush43 appointees, Tom Ridge and Michael Chertoff, condemned the federal action: "We reject a militarized response to protests to deny citizens their constitutional rights. Moreover, the blanket use of the label 'terrorists' to justify the use of paramilitary and military force is both factually wrong and legally unsupportable."

* * *

President Trump, however, could not alone successfully weaponize and leverage violence without his MAGA lieutenants. This angry army includes well-educated opportunists happy to scratch their authoritarian itch (Ted Cruz, Josh Hawley, Vivek Ramaswamy, and Ron DeSantis); most, in the estimation of Steven Levitsky and Daniel Ziblatt, coauthors of *How Democracies Die* and *Tyranny of the Minority*, are just "careerists—many were in the Capitol that day—who are simply trying to get ahead. But when democracy is at stake, choosing political ambition over its defense can be lethal."

- Roger Stone, Trump's longtime advisor, taunted Dems pre-Impeachment. "Just try it. You will have a spasm of violence in this country, an insurrection like you've never seen. Both sides are heavily armed, my friend. This is not 1974. People will not stand for Impeachment." Later, *Mediaite* released an audiotape of Stone actually suggesting to a NYPD officer the assassination of Democratic representatives Eric Swalwell and Jerrold Nadler, adding, "They need to get the message." In his defense, perhaps he was just being "fascetious."
- Ron DeSantis, trying to out-thug Trump, which isn't easy, chimed in that he would send in the American military to Mexico to go after drug cartels and would issue a "shoot-to-kill" order at the border and "shoot them stone-cold dead." He assailed the so-called "Deep State" with the explicit goal "to destroy leftism." The governor graphically added that "bureaucrats are going to be slitting their throats."
- Keri Lake, a Trump acolyte and occasional statewide candidate in Arizona, told an audience in 2023, "I have a message tonight for Merrick Garland and Jack Smith and Joe Biden. . . . If you want to get to President Trump, you are going to have go through me and 75 million Americans just like me. And most of us are card-carrying members of the NRA [National Rifle

Association]. That's not a threat, that's a public service announcement." The crowd cheered.

"Rhetoric like this has consequences," said Timothy J. Heaphy, the top investigator for the House Select Committee on January 6. "Politicians think that when they say things it's just rhetoric but people listen to it and take it seriously." This is especially obvious at Trump's rallies where content bias and groupthink make the angry audience seem to be one brain plugged into a single socket.

Based on his years running the FBI's counterintelligence program, Frank Figliuzzi agreed. "Trump's violence may lead to violence," he warned in mid-2022, because "his rants embold-ened white hate groups and racist blogs." Then just three days later, an El Paso gunman killed twenty-three Mexicans after posting a "manifesto" that repeatedly referred to Trump's inflammatory words and views. Indeed, *USA Today* found more than five hundred instances when Trump at rallies used words like "invasion," "predator," "killer," "criminal," and "animals" when discussing immigrants.

The *New York Times* finally weighed in with a passionate institutional editorial:

It is impossible to fully untangle the relationship between conspiracy theories and violence. But a survey this year found that some 18 million Americans believe that the 2020 election was stolen from Donald Trump and that force is justified to return him to power. Of those 18 million, eight million own guns, and one million either belong to a paramilitary group or know someone who does. That's alarming because violent people who belong to communities where violence is widely accepted are more likely to act. A portion of the G.O.P. has become such a community.

This is now commonly referred to as "stochastic terror," a term that came from the Greek word *stochastikos*, which the *Scientific American* defined this way: "Dehumanizing and vilifying a person or group of people can provoke what scholars and law enforcement officials call stochastic terrorism, in which ideologically driven hate speech increases the likelihood that people will violently and unpredictably attack the targets of vicious claims."

A conspiracy-minded Timothy McVeigh was the perpetrator of the 1995 Oklahoma City bombing that killed 168 people—the worst domestic terror attack in our history. Already infuriated by the Waco siege, he would regularly listen on long cross-country trips to talk-radio star Rush Limbaugh. "The second violent American Revolution," Rush would say, "is just about—I got my fingers about a quarter inch apart—is just about that far away." (McVeigh was executed; President Trump later awarded Limbaugh a Presidential Medal of Freedom during his last State of the Union address.)

Bill O'Reilly was even more explicit. He repeatedly said on his national radio show that "Tiller's a Killer" because Dr. George Tiller of Kansas performed lawful abortions. The doctor was then murdered in his church in 2009 by an antiabortion radical. More recently, after a President Trump tirade against the FBI, an armed man attacked an FBI headquarters in Cincinnati and was shot dead.

The same thing happened when the shooter at the Pittsburgh Tree of Life Synagogue and a different gunman at a Buffalo supermarket each spouted Trump-like racist rhetoric to explain their murder sprees. The assailant who bludgeoned Paul Pelosi in his San Francisco home had come to abduct Speaker Nancy Pelosi as "the leader of a pack of lying Democrats who were finally able to steal the election." Nine Michigan men—who called themselves "Wolverine Watchmen"—were convicted of attempting to kidnap and possibly murder Gov. Gretchen Whitmer over her COVID restrictions after President Trump had declared in a speech "Liberate Michigan!" Solomon Peña, a former Republican state legislature candidate in New Mexico, was arrested in 2022 for firing shots at the homes of various other lawmakers—and conspiring with would-be hit men—due to his conviction that the 2020 presidential election had been rigged.

As per usual, to escape blame for such stochastic violence, Republicans grasped for false equivalents. They repeatedly highlighted two octogenarians—Rep. Maxine Waters, a Black member from California, who once urged a small group of supporters to "confront" far-right opponents; and, after a Bernie Sanders supporter shot and seriously wounded Rep. Steve Scalise, parallels were drawn to far-left violence, although, of course, Sanders was not known for coaxing his progressive supporters to gun down bankers or Republicans.

Two conclusions: First, no one is saying that Trump bears criminal responsibility for inflammatory remarks later in time cited by murderers . . . but that he should be held morally and politically culpable because he, of course, understands the impact of his words on armed fanatical followers. These include both provocations ("will be wild!" he wrote to his huge online audience before January 6) and alibis (when asked about rioters chanting "Hang Mike Pence," he explained, "well, they were angry"). Second, at the very least, he and his supporters should condemn such assaults instead of a silence that can only serve as permission slips to future McVeighs. (A furious President George H. W. Bush, as one model, denounced the NRA after it called federal agents "jack-booted thugs.")

There must be a phrase beyond "shifting the Overton Window" to describe a president's claim that executive immunity allows him to kill opponents without suffering any criminal penalty and to explain how not one elected Republican condemned him for that fascist view. If that can't be called fascist, nothing can.

Guns and Crimes

A quarter century ago, a gunman entered Dunblane Primary School in Scotland, killing sixteen children and a teacher. A stunned United Kingdom quickly enacted very tight gun safety legislation. In the years since, there have been a total of zero school shootings in the country. And a month after a white supremacist in 2019 shot fifty to death in Wellington, New Zealand, an anti-terrorism law was enacted. In the United States, however, a 1994 law that reduced mass shootings by two-thirds was allowed to lapse in 2004 when George W. Bush was president. And within a week of the 2022 murder of nineteen children and a teacher in Uvalde, Texas, one House Republican—Rep. Timothy Burchett (R.-TN)—committed the gaffe of truth: "We're not gonna fix" gun laws.

Why the difference?

- Credit must first go to Justice Antonin Scalia for his ideological footwork. Although a unanimous 1934 decision found no constitutional right to own a firearm, Scalia in 2008 reinterpreted a comma in the Second Amendment to overturn two hundred years of constitutional law and basically neuter the phrase "well-regulated militia." The 5-4 opinion decided that laws in 1791 governing muskets—when there were no police forces and no AR-15s—should now apply to a country with more guns than people and twenty-five million semiautomatics. Talk about results-oriented judicial activism!

  Previously, former Chief Justice Warren E. Burger, appointed by President Nixon, denounced the theory that Scalia later adopted. "The Second Amendment has been the subject of one of the greatest pieces of fraud on the American public by special interests that I have ever seen in my lifetime," Burger said in retirement in 1991. "The very language of the Second Amendment refutes any argument that it was intended to guarantee every citizen an unfettered right to any kind of weapon he or she desires. The framers clearly intended to secure the right to bear arms essentially for military purposes."

  Nonetheless, the Thomas Six in 2022 expanded the Scalia revisionism, not the Burger refutation. In *New York Pistol and Gun Association,* a 6-3 Trump Court said the Second Amendment not only permitted individuals to have guns in their home but also to carry them wherever they went (as individuals, not in any "militia").

- After fifty-nine were shot to death in Las Vegas by a lone gunman with a semiautomatic, Bill O'Reilly admitted the calculus of expected death to his millions of radio listeners: "The Second Amendment is clear that Americans have a right to arm themselves for protection. Even the loons." Which translated means— tough luck kids since guns are their leading cause of death.
- After every mass shooting, GOP leaders— especially Gov. Greg Abbott of Texas, where many of them occur—blame "mental health" for these tragedies . . . which seems superficially plausible since killing children is an insane act. But just as auto safety began focusing not only on the "nut-behind-the-wheel" but also defective cars generally, the mental health alibi illogically erases the role of guns out of shootings. Since mental illness strikes a comparable percentage of people in the United States, Canada, and Norway (all about 24-27 percent), that political alibi cannot explain why gun deaths in Sweden were sixty and Canada three hundred, yet over thirty thousand in America.
- Second Amendment absolutists argue that it's wrong to punish "law-abiding citizens" with restrictions because of criminals. Adam Lanza was indeed law-abiding, right up to the day in 2012 when he stole his mother's semiautomatic and went into Sandy Hook Elementary School and murdered twenty-six people, twenty of whom were six and seven years old.
- The gun lobby also repeats that more guns equal more safety since they could be used to protect families from

invaders. But surveys show that it's six times more likely that such weapons are used against a family member (usually by accidental shootings) than against an intruder. Emma Fridel compared gun ownership rates and concealed carry laws in states from 1991 and 2016, finding that those with more guns and more lenient laws had 11 percent more gun deaths and 53 percent more mass shootings.

- Gun manufacturers and the NRA fetishize violence into a lifestyle in ads and slogans that especially attract young shooters. (See Ryan Busse's *Gunsight: My Battle Against the Industry that Radicalized America.*)

It's no surprise that between 1989 and 2022, according to OpenSecrets, gun groups contributed $50.5 million to GOP candidates and PACS—99 percent of all their giving.

Democrats take a decidedly different approach. They treat it as both a crime and a public health issue that should engage community groups, not merely something to run "tough on crime" ads against. (This more thoughtful theme helped Brandon Johnson get elected mayor of Chicago in 2023.) After horrific killings, as Republicans mumble about "thoughts and prayers," Biden and Democrats now invariably call for background checks for all gun purchases, state red flag laws, higher age requirements for all weapons and certainly for semiautomatics, and procurement that buys only technologically "safer" guns, as well as gun registration and liability insurance like what's required for cars.

Actual correlation studies could confirm what works and undermine years of gaslighting by a GOP saying anything to avoid a serious legislative debate. According to Dr. John J.

Donohue, a Stanford Law professor, it is possible to look at various studies and arrive at certain definite conclusions:

> Permissive laws about carrying of guns promote more gun violence than they deter and restrictions on assault weapons and high capacity magazines dampen mass shootings. Texas banned gun carrying from 1870 to 1995 before taking a very sharp pro-gun turn in 1996. The results? In 1995 Texas had about the level of homicide as New York, and California had a 25 percent higher murder rate than Texas. Today Texas has a 57.4 percent higher murder rate than New York and about an 18 percent higher murder rate than California. New York and California were restrictive on guns and benefited; Texas went the other way and has paid a bloody price. [While Trump describes urban America as scenes from the *Purge* movies, here are the murder rates per 100,000: NYC 5.3; US 5.5; Texas 8.2; Mississippi 23.7.]

But for now, Republicans will continue their obedience to Moloch, the ancient deity who demanded the sacrifice of children. Their indifference and cruelty can net votes for Democrats in the short run. But only some big cultural change—a 9/11-level tragedy involving guns or a national emergency declared by a forceful president—will lead to candidates fearing the wrath of voters more than of the gun lobby.

Fighting Violence with Law

One galvanizing issue dominated political conversations in the 1850s. Adherents on the two sides of slavery kept accelerating their threats of mutual violence until (a) a proslavery House Member went on the Senate floor and nearly caned to death the leading abolitionist of the day, Charles Sumner of Massachusetts, and (b) the antislavery religious zealot John Brown led a small group that attacked a garrison of Southern troops at Harpers Ferry in 1858 (led by Lt. Robert E. Lee) in a failed attempt to spark a slave revolt.

A century and a half later, a similar lineup of states and causes—not blue and gray but blue and red—are also creating an atmosphere of menace that has not risen to pre-1861 levels. But not for lack of trying.

Marjorie Taylor Greene had a private dinner with ex-president Trump in late 2023 to game out a possible impeachment of Joe Biden, with the goal, in her delirious words, to make him "lose big" in 2024 and endure a "long and excruciatingly painful" response. She also sparked calls for her own resignation after encouraging states to "consider seceding from the union" on the twenty-second anniversary of the 9/11 terror attacks due to "Biden's traitorous America-last border policies."

That same week, Georgia state senator Colton Moore suggested that civil war could break out over the prosecution of Donald Trump in his state. "We've got nineteen people who are facing the rest of their life in prison because they spoke out against an election," Moore said in an appearance on Steve Bannon's *War Room* podcast. "We've got to figure this out because, if we don't, our constituencies are going to be fighting in the streets. Do you want a civil war? I don't want a civil war. I don't want to have to draw my rifle." On cue, Trump retweeted and lauded "the highly respected Georgia State Senator who deserves thanks and congratulations for having the courage and conviction to fight the radical-left lunatics."

Worst is Texas Governor Greg Abbott, who is methodically poking the federal bear as he barb-wires the border to deter or kill migrants. Even after the Trump Supreme Court decided narrowly to maintain the two-hundred-year-old "Supremacy Clause" in early 2024, Abbott proposed using the Texas National Guard unless the DHS stepped up its game. As if it were April 1861, twenty-five GOP state attorneys general seconded his call and considered sending their national guards. Brilliant. Do they know who won the first and so far only Civil War?* But while it's impossible to know the upshot of all such incendiary talk as of early 2024, we know that the violent Right will refuse to accept any blame for the domestic terrorism it inspires. For now, they are holding America hostage to their vow to make sure that we stick to our guns so that we retain our right from 1789 to own a musket.

When it comes to the kind of violence common to authoritarian countries, the GOP appears intent on triggering or tolerating political violence—like how Trump invariably puts the addresses and personal information of critics and prosecutors on his Truth Social site knowing that a wave of death threats will ensue. He fully understands and is willing to deploy his leverage to frighten and silence potential critics. Little wonder

---

* For what it's worth, the writer does not think that a new Civil War is likely. But every time that the Glenn Becks, Marjorie Taylor Greenes, and Colton Moores keep the speculation up, it (a) raises funds for whomever is talking, and (b) makes it seem less insane and inconceivable. And it does increase the risk that, should Trump lose, there would be not organized state-on-state violence but hundreds of individual armed attacks by local Far-Right radicals and militia.

that Judge Lewis Kaplan, at the conclusion of the E. Jean Carroll defamation trial, told jurors, "If I were you, I wouldn't tell anyone that I was on this jury." Has there ever been such a judicial suggestion other than perhaps a mob trial?

The phrase for this is domestic terrorism.

INSERT II
WOKE'S A JOKE

If all else fails, Republicans cling to this one-word howitzer. Proponents just aim it at any policy they want to disparage—the "woke military," "woke history," "woke banks"—which relieves the speaker of having to provide any real supporting evidence. So you can imply something is sinister without actually saying it.

There's a method to their badness. Right-wing propagandist Chris Rufo, for a prominent example, is credited with kidnapping the word "woke"—which only a few years ago was Black slang meaning someone "who gets it"—to now imply that looney liberals are supposedly "anti-white."

Often Republicans can't even describe this verbal pillar of their party. Dana Perino on Fox admitted that she couldn't "define it in a *Webster's Dictionary* sense; it could be a feeling, a sense." (Shades of Justice Potter Stewart on pornography—"You know it when you see it.")

From critical race theory, DEI (diversity, equity, and inclusion), grooming, gay marriage, gas stoves, pronouns, the Wuhan Lab, the Deep State, War on Xmas, Bud Light, Disney, and *Barbie* (!), nearly all Republicans have cited them as "Woke" from time to time. In Nikki Haley's fervid estimate, they add up to "a virus more dangerous than the pandemic."

Whoa. Can these partisans elevate them guns a little lower?

"Woke" is a manufactured word to imply that something or someone is a phony if they believe in social justice and racial tolerance. (So do users of the word therefore *favor* social injustice and racial bigotry?) Replace WOKE instead with "liberal" or the "N" word and it's easy to see that it's merely age-old whine in new bottles.

> Here's ex-Joint Chiefs of Staff Mark Milley to *The Atlantic:* "The military wasn't woke 24 months ago and now it's woke? You want woke? Here's what your military is doing: there are 5000 sorties a day, including patrols protecting the USA and our interests around the world. We have 250,000 troops overseas in 140 countries defending the rules-based order. Our readiness statuses are at the highest levels they've been in 20 years. So this idea of a woke military is total, utter, made-up bullshit"

Nor is "WOKE" their only rhetorical trick. When lacking arguments in policy exchanges, Republicans resort to a rotating blur of lies, linguistic hijinks, rhetorical questions, false accusations, and hot adjectives (see chapter "The Lyin' Kings") to gaslight their biased base. These comprise, according to ex-Republican Nicolle Wallace on MSNBC, "a hamster on a wheel that never gets the cheese" because there's always a new *scandal du jour* to grab attention when earlier ones fall from the headlines.

CHAPTER 4
A PARTY OF CORRUPTION—
"We Don't Care"

People have been thrown in jail for several years for try-ing to counterfeit one vote yet, according to Trump's law-yers, if he tried to counterfeit or steal an entire election, he was just exercising his First Amendment rights. That's deranged.

—**Rep. Jamie Raskin**

It's time to stop appeasing the fascists among us. . . . Don't say that we should look forward, not back. . . . Appeasement is what got us to where we are. It has to stop, now.

—**Paul Krugman**

A Massive Fraud of this magnitude [supposedly "stealing the election"] allows for the termination of all rules, regu-lations and articles, even those found in the Constitution.

—**Donald Trump**

There's corruption in both parties (in this decade, incarcer-ated governors range from Rod R. Blagojevich (D.-IL) to

John G. Rowland (R.-CT). But the party known to venerate the profit-making private sector and disdain public service not unexpectedly has more politicians with bigger police blotters. Here are the number of indictments under modern presidents (worst four in italics all Republican):

Obama: zero
Ford: one
Carter: one
Bush 41: one
Clinton: two
Bush 43: sixteen
Reagan: twenty-six
Nixon: seventy-six
Trump: ninety-one

Using the criterion of *convictions,* Team Trump's felons to date include his: campaign chair; deputy campaign chair; personal lawyer; several lawyers in his various criminal trials; longest-term political strategist; National Security advisor; foreign policy advisor; CFO of the Trump Organization; with a dozen others now pending trial. This doesn't even include his proven culpability for defamation, financial fraud, and rape.

Like DiMaggio's fifty-six-game hitting streak, that's a record unlikely to ever be broken.

In the modern era, Republicans have a poor record on corruption and character. Joe McCarthy's name stands out as a demagogue falsely accusing people of communist associations. Dennis Hastert, the longest-serving Republican House Speaker in history, was convicted of sexual child abuse and served eighteen months in prison. Richard Nixon, until recently, was the most corrupt American president—though he was famously pardoned by his successor Gerald Ford, Nixon's scandal sent twenty-nine aides to jail, including two attorneys general and his top two White House deputies. (This number does not include what conservative columnist George Will called "treason" by Nixon for secretly encouraging the Viet Cong to torpedo the Paris Peace talks just before the 1968 Election.)

When three years later Nixon said that "if the president does it, that means that it is not illegal," it was universally rejected as an endorsement of dictatorship over a constitutional republic.

Yet now a half century later comes Donald Trump and a MAGA Party with newer attempts at political self-acquittal, despite multiple bookings on felony charges. It was awkward that the self-proclaimed party of "Law and Order" rhetorically and repeatedly shouted "Lock her up" in 2016 about Hillary Clinton (who was never charged) yet are now exclaiming *witch hunt* as real courts assess guilt or innocence.

It's a modern rendition of the classic film *The Hunchback of Notre Dame.* When someone comments on the huge lump on his back, he responds in mock bewilderment, "What hump?"

That stonewalling won't work again given his proven history and character. So the 2024 election will be less about MAGA policy than whether voters would elect a Republican president who is being daily exposed as engaged in a multilevel criminal conspiracy—spreading lies about voter fraud, organizing sedition, pressuring the Department of Justice to pretend it was investigating Biden, pressuring state officials to send fake electors, obstructing justice—and now trying to

escape the long-arm of the law, which could forever subjugate
law to politics.

It's the rule of law or "What Hump?"

HISTORY: *"A Shocking Pattern of Illegality"*

Trump is the unique offspring of his mentor Roy Cohn and
father Fred. Cohn was the unctuous fixer who whispered in
McCarthy's ear, and who was later disbarred and became the
twisted protagonist in Tony Kushner's acclaimed *Angels in
America*. Fred was a Queens wheeler-dealer who brought up
his favored son based on one ethic: in any business or political
transaction, as reported by niece Mary Trump, he would actually tell his son, "you must be a killer! a killer! a killer!"

There are scores of cases pre-presidency that reveal his
corrupt mentality—so many it's hard to remember any in particular. To jog the memory of those who try to brush off his
illegality since "they all do it," consider this rap sheet:

- *"C"*: The very first time Donald's name appeared
  in the *New York Times* was in September 1973 when
  Nixon's Justice Department and Housing and Urban
  Development (HUD) sued father and son for willfully
  excluding African American applicants from their
  housing units by designating their paperwork with
  the code letter "C" (for "colored"). After countersuing
  the DOJ in a pure Cohn middle-finger maneuver, they
  promised to discontinue the practice. But they didn't
  end it and had to be sued again on the same grounds
  in 1978 and again promised in a new consent decree to
  knock it off.

- **Trump "University":** After a NYS Attorney General lawsuit found seven thousand victims paying up to $35,000 each for promised teachers and courses that didn't materialize, Trump blustered that he would never settle the 2015 case "because you get known as a settler." By which he meant that he'd settle just after the 2016 presidential election and the week before a scheduled jury trial, agreeing to pay $25 million in restitution.
- **Trump "Foundation":** After he called the Clinton Foundation a crooked enterprise despite its "A" rating from the American Institute of Philanthropy, state AG Barbara Underwood sued the Trump Foundation in 2018 "for being little more than a checkbook to serve Mr. Trump's business and political interests [in a] shocking pattern of illegality" (like spending $10,000 on a portrait of himself that he displayed at his golf facilities).

  In 2019, he paid another $25 million, dissolved the "Foundation," and promised that neither he nor his family would serve on any foundation board of directors for ten years. Consequently, that year he was allowed to run for reelection as president of the United States but not for the board of directors of any New York charitable enterprise.
- **TrumpToo.** After nearly sixty women publicly accused him of sexual assault—many chronicled in Barry Levin and Monique El-Faizy's *All the President's Women*— Trump called them "horrible, horrible liars" and threatened to sue them all once the 2020 race was over.

(He sued none, though writer E. Jean Carroll brought two defamation lawsuits and was awarded nearly $90 million in restitution and penalties.) Chris Christie framed the situation nicely: "I mean, he must be the unluckiest S.O.B. in the world. He just has random people he's never met before who were able to convince a jury that he sexually abused them. I mean, this guy, it's one person after another, one woman after another."

- **Tax Fraud.** An extensive investigation by the *New York Times* in April 2019 documented how Trump family members created a shell company that enabled them to fake invoices to hide gifts and charge rents higher than allowed in their residential buildings. The Pulitzer Prize–winning investigation forced Trump's sister, the late federal judge Maryanne Trump Barry, to quickly resign in the face of formal judicial inquiries into her role.

PRESIDENCY

Of course there's a presumption of innocence in criminal cases until a defendant is found guilty beyond a reasonable doubt . . . because American courtrooms can't sentence someone to prison based on unproven allegations. But in the arena of politics, candidates regularly accuse others of misconduct since what is at stake is losing not your liberty but merely an election. Indeed, given Trump's lifelong run-ins with the law and with the truth, there should probably be a rebuttable journalistic presumption of corruption in any controversy.

Since coverage of his pending major cases is so extensive— and new incriminating evidence comes out daily—there's little need for this book to explore in detail the charges and evidence in each. But a quick scorecard can be useful for those who may have succumbed to scandal fatigue. This is what we know as of early 2024, with many verdicts to come:

- **The Stormy Daniels/Election Interference case** alleges that Trump paid off porn star Stormy Daniels by altering business records to buy her silence just before the 2016 general election. It's open-and-shut that (a) Trump signed the $270,000 in checks (most in the Oval Office!) that paid her off and (b) middleman Michael Cohen was found guilty and imprisoned for participating in the same scheme with "Individual #1," which DA Alvin Bragg now considers "election interference." A trial is set for March 25.
- **The "Willful Retention [a.k.a. "theft"] of National Security information"** Despite repeated attempts by the government to retrieve them and then a lawful warrant to search his Florida home, Trump held onto classified information that his own lawyer, Jennifer Little, told him would be criminal if he kept it hidden. While over half of Republicans in polls say he never kept such material, Trump himself admitted it in various recorded conversations and interviews. As for his constant refrain that he had every right to take whatever documents he wanted, the Presidential Records Act said the opposite: "The Federal Government shall reserve and retain complete ownership, possession and control of President Records."

(Compare this squalid behavior on a national security matter with his comment in the 2016 campaign that "In my administration, I'm going to enforce all laws concerning the protection of classified information. No one is above the law.")

- **Special Counsel Jack Smith indicted Trump for obstructing an official proceeding** based on hard evidence that he arm-twisted VP Mike Pence to refuse to perform his constitutional duty to certify the vote on January 6 and strived to get members of Congress to object too. (Pence didn't; but a breathtaking two-thirds of GOP House members did object a few hours after being attacked by a Trump mob at their place of work.) The goal was to deny Biden the 270 electoral college votes needed to win and thereby throw the election to the House of Representatives, as happened in 1800 and 1876, so that state delegations could select the president. (In 2020, that would have meant Trump.) The ex-president's attempt to dismiss the case due to "presidential immunity" even after he left office foundered on the ridiculous premise that the nation's chief law enforcer could violate the law, as a unanimous three-judge panel of the DC Court of Appeals— including one Trump appointee—concluded.

- **Fulton County, Georgia DA Fani Willis brought a racketeering conspiracy charge** against Trump and eighteen others for trying to overturn the results of the 2020 election. Counts included Trump's famous phone call asking Secretary of State Brad Raffensperger to "find 11,780 votes" so he could claim victory as well as an attempt to create fake electors to try to deny Biden his electoral college majority. The 161 actions taken in furtherance of the alleged conspiracy revealed an extensive plot. Several defendants pled guilty before a likely court date for the others in mid-2024.

- *NY Attorney General Letitia James brought a civil fraud case in 2018* based on the allegation that Trump cooked the books to pay less in taxes and get paid more for assets that the company sold. A civil court found that he did engage in extensive fraud and imposed a fine of some $450 million (with interest) as well as barred Trump and sons from doing business in New York for three years. And the sitting judge called their complete lack of contrition almost "pathological."

- *Fake Electors* in Wisconsin and Arizona tried to use forged documents to replace bona fide Biden electors in order to get the election thrown to the House of Representatives. Twelve defendants in Wisconsin admitted to the scheme, pled guilty, and publicly acknowledged that Biden did not steal their state's presidential election. (The Arizona case—which includes the state's GOP chairman as a defendant—is still pending.)

- *Despite a constitutional ban on receiving "emoluments,"* Trump repeatedly milked his office for personal or family gain, which was consistent with his earlier statement as a candidate that he could "both run the country and my business as well . . . but I won't do that." Wrote one wag on Twitter in 2023: "Explosive new reporting revealed that Hunter Biden

cleared a whopping $640 million as an advisor to the
White House . . . Just kidding—that was Jared and
Ivanka."

Indeed, the final amount was emolumentally greater
since Mohammed bin Salman Al Saud (MBS), Saudi's
Arabia's undisputed leader whom Jared befriended
through his White House position, returned the favor
by overruling his financial advisors to provide a cool
$2 billion—two-thirds of the total raised—to underwrite
Kushner's new venture capital fund. (Trump and several
courts delayed several serious cases brought against
him based on the constitutional prohibition of such
rewards, until they became moot when he left office.)

Despite an avalanche of false allegations by House
Republicans that "the Biden family" received enormous
sums from foreign countries, House Oversight ranking
Democrat Jamie Raskin disclosed in early 2024 that,
mirabile dictu, Trump earned nearly $8 million from
several foreign governments, mostly China, to create
the first "for-profit presidency."

- *The 1939 Hatch Act* prohibits using federal workers
  and facilities to engage in partisan activity, which
  Trump frequently and blatantly did—such as
  announcing his candidacy for reelection on the very
  grounds of the White House. When his presidential
  team worried that they might be violating a federal law,
  he responded with a Full Nixon: "And who decides on
  Hatch Act violations? Me. Do what you want."
- *Section III of the Fourteenth Amendment
  specifically disqualifies* any federal officer who took

an oath to support the Constitution from holding office if they "aided or abetted" an "insurrection or rebellion against the United States." The state of Colorado held a five day hearing which found that Trump was an Insurrectionist under the literal text of this post-Civil War Amendment. Trump declared the best thing to do was let voters decide in Fall 2024, except that's precisely what he wouldn't allow voters to do in 2020 once he lost. "It's the Constitution disqualifying him, not Biden, not Democrats, not never-Trumps," concluded retired Judge J. Michael Luttig, comparing it to other clear disqualifications like being too young or not a natural-born citizen.

Oral arguments, however, focused not on the great fear that traitors might get back in power but rather on (a) procedural minutiae like whether the president was an "office" under the Constitution, (b) hypothetical horrors about how bad-faith actors might misuse application of the plain text of the Section, and (c) why only one state might decide such a momentous question as Disqualification than, say, the Congress.*

---

* Roberts/Gorsuch/Alito focused not on the jugular but the capillaries: it skipped by the extreme threats to democracy of Reconstruction and January 6; it treated seriously the question of whether the nation's top elected politician was an oath-taking "official" (which all middle-schoolers could answer); it worried about a state having undue influence yet ignored that, in fact, a majority of both the House and Senate had already concluded the Trump was an insurrectionist in his second Impeachment and trial; and as Nation legal analyst Elie Mystal explained, "they were more concerned with a Red state legislature and Governor kicking Biden off the ballot for bad-faith reasons than they were kicking Trump off for good-faith reasons. 'But, what might Ron DeSantis do' is not a good way to run a country."

The Court appears very likely to allow Trump to stay on the ballot. It looks probable that November will indeed prove to be "the Inflection Election."

* * *

The impressive breadth of all the charges and allegations against Trump make him an historical figure on a scale between Benedict Arnold and one hundred Nixons. But as a showman, Trump keenly understands the political need to say *something* in response to all these charges, at a minimum to hold onto his cult of the sincerely irrational. Here are some of the excuses for his predatory behavior that, to be honest, are about as convincing as anything in the "dog-ate-my-homework" category:

- He called the varied prosecutors pursuing him—including three who were Black—"racists" and implied that urban areas like Atlanta and New York City were too racially hostile to him to be fair.
- When confronted with disclosures of Trump saying or doing something indefensible, his default position would be to claim that it was "a joke . . . locker-room talk. . . bravado" etc. He'd then escape accountability by making the defense of Lewis Carroll's Humpty Dumpty that "When I use a word, it means just what I choose it to mean—neither more nor less."
- Trumpers discounted the Bragg/Hush Money case as small potatoes. But buying Stormy Daniels's silence after the *Access Hollywood* tape ("if you're a star, they let you

do it") arguably *did* save his candidacy by making sure that voters weren't reminded about his infidelity in the campaign's final week. Which is big potatoes.

- Senator Lindsay Graham first warned that, if Trump were indicted for anything, riots would erupt throughout the country (he was and they didn't). After Mark Meadows made a phone call to another named coconspirator in the Atlanta RICO prosecution, Fox anchors emphasized that making a phone call is legal. So is mailing a letter . . . unless it's the Unabomber using that method of communication to include lethal explosives. Context counts.

Not known as typical ACLU members previously, many MAGAs pressed the case that free speech allowed Trump to say what he wanted at the Washington Ellipse on January 6 and in phone conversations with his lawyers. But if a free-speech defense was valid, there would be no conspiracy prosecutions and no libel, defamation, bribery, child pornography, or blackmail cases either, all of which turn on incriminating words and messages.

- Some Trumpers initially claimed that January 6 wasn't an Insurrection but "a tourist visit" and/or a mob of Antifa activists egged on by the FBI. To date, not one of the 1,200 insurrectionists convicted of January 6-related crimes—nor anyone else—has implicated the FBI or Antifa members. And, of course, the bureau is famously about the most culturally conservative bunch of white men in the US government.

- He claimed to have issued a standing order to declassify whatever White House documents he took home, and/or it was good enough that he simply telepathically "think" declassification for it to occur. Except neither his vice president nor chief of staff recalled such an order. And while showing classified documents to an aide and journalist at his Bedminster home in 2021, Trump is heard on tape saying, "As president, I could have declassified it. Now I can't."

- The Mueller Report in 2019 ended with Trump mocking its allegations of collusion as "Russia, Russia, Russia." But in fact those prosecutors did charge twenty-six Russian nationalists, three Russian companies, and six Trump associates with crimes, obtaining four convictions of the latter group (including campaign manager Paul Manafort). It was AG Bill Barr who functioned as the tip of the spear that month by refusing to consider ten Obstruction of Justice charges laid out in the final report and whose public dismissal ("no collusion") of the section on Russia was, according to a federal judge, "deceptive and misleading."

  A later report by the Center for American Progress documented that his campaign and Russians had 238 contacts and thirty-eight meetings during the election. Stuart Stevens, a Republican strategist and previously Mitt Romney's campaign manager, called a spade a spade on MSNBC: "In 2016, nearly all intelligence agencies and professionals concluded that Russia had a campaign to elect Donald Trump. He won. What did they get? The anti-Soviet and anti-Russian Republican party then became the home of Putin in America. I think that was the most successful covert operation ever by a hostile foreign power."

- Perhaps you've heard that Trump dismissed every single charge against him as a "witch hunt" or "hoax" (the exact words that Nixon and his VP Spiro Agnew had also used, before both resigned) and most of his supporters glibly regard pending criminal cases as merely "weaponized justice." Except it was neither Biden nor Merrick Garland but independent special counsels—and unanimous grand juries—that brought cases sustained by reams of public evidence.

In fact, Trump's entire strategy of victimhood is belied by the reality that (a) many of the judges ruling against him in his sixty losing civil cases were appointed by Republican presidents, including himself; (b) they based their decisions in part on his own attorney general's conclusion in late December 2020 that "there was no significant fraud that altered the outcome;" and (c) nearly all of the witnesses before the House January 6 Committee who first made the public case for his culpability were Republicans. Also, here is Trump biographer David C. Johnston: "A federal judge (appointed by Trump) issued a search warrant at the request of the director of the FBI (appointed by Trump) and he was charged under a law (passed by Trump)."

All his arguments add up to the conclusion that Republicans can lose the popular vote yet still be awarded the election and shouldn't be tried in a blue state or a city with too many Black people.*

Imagine if Jimmy Carter or Barack Obama had been credibly accused of fifty-five crimes (as CREW concluded Trump was in his presidency)—or even one. Fox would chew on that bone for years. And despite his blizzard of alibis, no Trump supporter should get away with blasé recitals of conspiracies and denials. For we do know based on court settlements and judicial opinions that he in fact did defraud banks and Trump U. students, did steal White House documents when he left and refused to return them, did assault numerous women, including E. Jean Carroll. And rape her, in the "common use" of that term, according to Judge Lewis Kaplan. So a person who announced his candidacy by condemning Mexico for sending us rapists *is* one.

And now, zero remorse. His Brown Shirts are no different. "The Court is accustomed to defendants who refuse to accept they did anything wrong," wrote Judge Royce Lamberth, a Reagan appointee and senior federal district court judge, about

---

* Projection much? His loud accusations of "voter fraud" served to cover up the reality—which hasn't yet been understood by his army of grunts—that nearly all those recently convicted of political offenses have been *Republicans:* like the four seniors in The Villages in Florida who pled guilty to voting twice, three of them Republicans for Trump; an ex-speaker in Michigan who admitted he took $110,000 in bribes to direct marijuana licenses to allies; a former top aide to Mitch McConnell and Rand Paul who was convicted of helping a Russian illegally funnel a political donation to Trump's 2016 campaign; state senator Brian Kelsey (R.-TN) who was given a twenty-one-month prison sentence for campaign finance violations; Alabama state representative David Cole charged last August with voter fraud; and, most astonishingly, Charles McGonigal—the ex-head of counterintelligence for the FBI in NY who had helped convince Director Comey to reopen the "emails case" against Hillary—who plead guilty to taking money from Oleg Derespoka, widely called "Putin's Oligarch." It appears that Russia *was* "listening."

January 6 defendants. "But in my 37 years on the bench, I cannot recall a time when such meritless justifications of criminal activity have gone mainstream."

RUDY: *"Either you love him . . . or he hates you."*

If there were an avatar of Trumpism, it would be the person who was Trump before Trump. In his public life, Giuliani has been a relentless bully who operated on the core ethic of Machiavelli's *The Prince*—"better to be feared than loved." When mayor of New York City, he would sit with top aides on New Year's Day and rewatch *The Godfather* (I and II). This was the storyline that guided him to become a venerated prosecutor, mob-slayer, scourge of Wall Street, "America's Mayor," knighted hero of 9/11, and consigliere to a president.

Yet he ended up arrested in Atlanta on August 24, 2023, on RICO charges under a law he famously pioneered as US Attorney. His corrupt character, however, like Trump's, began far earlier than his public disgrace.

He grew up in a Catholic enclave in Flatbush, Brooklyn, where his father (later imprisoned for six months as a mob enforcer who robbed a milkman at gunpoint) taught him to box at two to prepare for a harsh world outside their modest environs. Under the guidance of a doting mother, he would listen rapt for hours to operas resonant with great battles between good (him) and evil (others). As a young boy, he'd periodically look into mirrors saying "I, Rudolph Wilson Giuliani, do solemnly swear" in anticipation of the day he'd take the presidential oath of office. The result was a driven pugilist who, as his top aide later told the author, "woke up every morning as mayor looking to pick a fight he could win."

That often meant me. For on the same day in November 1993 that he narrowly defeated David Dinkins to become mayor, I was elected the citywide Public Advocate for NYC, the office next in line to the mayor whose job was to oversee him . . . "oversight" being regarded as a communicable disease to aspiring authoritarians.

His eight-year tenure was marred by numerous violations of laws and norms.

- Amateur photographer James Schillaci complained to the NYPD about a radar trap in front of the Bronx Zoo. Getting no response, he appealed to my office, and we persuaded the *Daily News* to expose it on their front page. An outraged Giuliani had him arrested and handcuffed at his home for a thirteen-year-old outstanding traffic warrant (which was soon dropped as dated). Then the NYPD released a list of arrests going back fourteen years, including a false accusation of sodomy.

  According to a *New York Times* account, "he was briefly hospitalized and later received a $290,000 legal settlement from the City." Columnist Jim Dwyer of the *Daily News* wrote about this David-Goliath, "This isn't police brutality—it is mayoral brutality."
- When it came to the law, Giuliani, like his friend Donald Trump, treated it as an annoyance. After an innocent Black vendor, Patrick Dorismond, was shot and killed in a police scuffle on the West Side in 2000, the mayor disparaged the victim as "no altar boy" and released his juvenile records. Except he *had* been an altar boy

(at Giuliani's own Catholic high school no less), and, as a court held in a case filed by the author, it was unlawful to leak such confidential records.

- He had a terrible relationship with the Black community, starting as far back as 1989 when he egged on a couple thousand protesting cops—many shouting the "N" word in what came to be called "a police riot"— on the steps of City Hall over the creation of a Civilian Complaint Review Board. In office, he refused to meet with many major Black officials for years, and later told an audience that candidate Barack Obama "doesn't love America like we do."

- Planning to run for the US Senate in 1998 against Hillary Clinton, he put a public referendum on the ballot to take the office of Public Advocate out of the line of succession—a two-fer to keep me from the mayoralty should he have won and kneecapping a rival. His audacious and outrageous proposal lost by 3-1 in a public vote.

Giuliani's life as a reverse Lincoln—"with malice toward all and charity for none"—resulted in two disbarments (in NYC and DC), two indictments related to Fake Electors and obstruction of justice on January 6, as well as Ukraine-related misconduct that directly led to President Trump being twice impeached in separate episodes by the House of Representatives.

When arraigned on his first indictment, he reverted to his jaunty, scornful personality, asserting to the scrum of reporters that "if they can do this to me, they can do it to anyone." Which was certainly true if the "anyone" was also someone who tried to overthrow the government they had taken an oath to uphold. A few months later, a financial hammer fell when a civil jury found him liable for $148 million for defamation of two Black election workers who he repeatedly and falsely accused of altering vote totals, which led to a gusher of racial abuse and death threats. Asked at a House January 6 Committee hearing what she was afraid of, the adult daughter answered, "my son finding me and my mom hanging from a tree."

Now facing bankruptcy if not prison, Giuliani is the operatic story of hubris—of a moth drawn to fame. Other than Harvey Weinstein, Bill Cosby, and O. J. Simpson, has anyone fallen further from toast of the town to toast than Giuliani?

END GAME: *Trump "Fought the Law and the Law Won."*

Numerous observers from James Comey, Michael Cohen, Michael Wolfe, and Jake Sullivan have compared Trump to a mobster, in both aspects of the word: he could inflame a mob and imitate a mob boss by his use of intimidation. But as *The Atlantic* cheekily observed, that comparison risked "insulting mob bosses everywhere." Funny but not entirely untrue. At a White House holiday party that year, top Trump aide Dan Scavino told Counsel Jenna Ellis, "the boss is not going to leave under any circumstances. We are just going to stay in power." When even loyalist Ellis explained that that's not how the law works, Scavino replied, "We don't care."

Trump does best when he isolates each accusation one by one so he can pretend that each one is some kind of exception or persecution. The value of looking at them holistically is that can spotlight his multifaceted criminal conspiracy to stay in power: sixty civil lawsuits; pressure on the DOJ to simply say they've began a major probe of voter fraud; fake electors plus arm-twisting state election officials; the Insurrection; and pressure on Pence to violate his oath of office. It's not so much one thing as the whole thing—a conspiracy to illegally seize power.

As of February 15, he's barely one step ahead of the sheriff. With implausible appeals pending, he's been hit with about $540 million in penalties even before the IRS completes an audit that could reach $100 million and before wrongful death and injury cases are heard from House and police victims on Jan. 6. At this rate, he may well end up, to use Gail Collins's taunt of his Croatian claims, "a thousand-aire."

But now that criminal court dates are being set, Trump is running out of legal options. One is the fantastically big idea of reelection and then self-pardon, which is Hail Mary pass territory. The other are his familiar combination of legal delays and hints of violence that tripped up people who failed to hold him accountable at various key moments—Mueller (assisted by Barr), Garland, McConnell, and McCarthy. Unlike them, however, Jack Smith, Fani Willis, Alvin Bragg, and Letitia James do not appear likely to go wobbly. Cinematically, they're more like the very focused posse of sheriffs near the end of *Butch Cassidy and the Sundance Kid* chasing down the two antiheroes. Finally, an anxious and exhausted Paul Newman turns to Robert Redford and asks, "who *are* those guys?"

CHAPTER 5
LOATHE THY NEIGHBOR:
Republicans and Race

Segregation is not a disease of the colored but of white people.

—**Albert Einstein**, 1946

If you can convince the lowest white man he's better than the best colored man, he won't notice you're picking his pocket. Hell, give him somebody to look down on, and he'll empty his pockets for you.

—**President Lyndon Johnson**

BLM is definitely not about Black Lives and remember that when they come for you.

—**Tucker Carlson**

"Who won the Civil War?"

Even Florida textbooks would (reluctantly) answer—the North won, Slavery lost, and Blacks became American citizens. But in countless ways since 1865, America is still fighting over their second-class citizenship, the result of a tragic campaign of violence during Reconstruction by Confederate remnants to restore their "heritage." When the hope for a better postwar South ran into a failed Reconstruction—a direct result of the assassination of the sixteenth president—it proved to be the most significant inflection moment for American society, at least until now.

For in 2024, that tragedy has culminated in a modern Republican Party that alternates between race-baiting to win votes and trying to erase race altogether from public discourse. In Trump Land, even discussing racism is called racist, as if a tumor will go away if you ignore it.

Let's be adults. Here are four well-documented ways that Donald Trump has dug his fingers into the wound of race to brainwash MAGAs and win white votes: he pushed the fantastic lie for years that an American president—who happened to be the first Black POTUS—was not an American; at his 2015 presidential announcement, he said that Mexicans were "rapists" and thereafter frequently compared immigrants to animals "invading America"; he repeatedly mocked House members of color as radical, corrupt, and stupid people who should "go back" to their countries of origin; and he and his party can't stop trying to reduce the number of minorities who vote.

"If that's the essence of your entire political identity," said renowned Black author Ta-Nehisi Coates, in studied understatement, "you might be a White Supremacist."

HISTORY OF THE FAR WHITE

When Team Trump reaches for its first line of defense on race—*"are you calling Donald Trump and the Republican Party racist?"*—don't flinch. *"Of course we are, if we include complicit GOP careerists who just go along to get along."*

Then go to the videotape.

Trump

As noted earlier, his father Fred was arrested at a 1927 Ku Klux Klan rally in Queens. Cut to 1973 and 1978 when the Nixon administration twice had to sue the Trump Organization (both Fred and Donald) for excluding minorities from their residential housing units. (When a Black nurse filled out a form that met all the criteria for a lease, the company agent asked Fred what to do with it. "Take the application and put it in a drawer and leave it there.")

After a notorious attack on a white female jogger in Central Park in April 1989, five Black teenagers were arrested and charged. In what was his first public policy statement, developer Donald Trump left his familiar world of square feet and mortgage rates to run full-page ads in all four NYC newspapers with the headline "Bring Back the Death Penalty!" The suspects were convicted of rape but not executed . . . and ten years later their convictions were set aside by DA Robert Morgenthau due to coerced confessions. Trump called their exoneration "the heist of the century." (Instead of ashes in an urn, one just got elected as the City Councilman from Harlem.)

When asked to criticize David Duke's racism during his 2016 presidential campaign, Trump begged off, feigning ignorance about the most notorious racist in the country: "I know nothing about David Duke, I know nothing about white supremacists." As president, according to his then lawyer Michael Cohen, "he told me that Black people would never vote for him because they were too stupid." And he was quoted in *This Week* saying, "I've got Black accountants counting my money. I hate it! . . . I think that guy's lazy and it's probably not his fault because laziness is a trait of Blacks."

Give him points for candor and consistency—Trump's racial taunts are hard to miss. He called Rep. Maxine Waters "an extraordinarily low-IQ person" and periodically denounced prominent Black female journalists—Yamiche Alcindor, April Ryan, Abby Phillip—for asking "stupid . . . racist questions." He wanted to stop immigration of Muslims generally or at least from certain Muslim countries (unaware of or indifferent to a Constitution hostile to "religious tests"). He frequently disparaged countries with large Black populations as "shitholes" and wondered out loud about US immigration policy, "Why do we need Haitians? We should have more people from places like Norway." (Norway is 86 percent white; 5.1 percent Black.)

He infamously couldn't condemn neo-Nazis demonstrating in Charlottesville to keep Confederate statues in public places without also blathering about "fine people on both sides." And late in the 2020 campaign, he warned "women in the suburbs" that a Biden win would increase integrated housing. "You know who's going to be in charge of HUD? Cory Booker." Why that choice of senator? Here's the translation for any who might be confused: *Run for your lives; Democrats and Blacks are coming!*

Little surprise then that Americans considered him racist by 51 to 45 percent in a Quinnipiac Poll before the 2020 General Election (in 1968, 41 percent thought that segregationist George Wallace was.)

Republicans

During and after the Civil War, proslavery Democrats were the majority party in the Confederate states. Indeed, a century later, Nixon was competitive for the Black vote (at least until JFK called an anxious Coretta Scott King when her husband was in an Alabama jail). Half of Senate Republicans even voted in favor of the 1964 Civil Rights Act.

But that historic habit ended during one of the two greatest political realignments in our history (1932 being the other), when gobsmacked Southern whites finally realized that Northern liberals were to blame for the Civil Rights Acts of the 1960s. Barry Goldwater, who opposed the 1964 Public Accommodations Act, won five Southern states in 1964.

Alarmed by the reduction of the Caucasian population by 8.6 percent this century (224 million to 204 million), the white working-class vote went Republican by nearly 70 percent in each of the past six presidential elections. *Politico* reports that in 2020, Trump won an astonishing 96 percent of districts where at least 70 percent of the people were white and also fewer than 30 percent college educated.

Unarguably, the Republican Party is now the party of white voters, and the Democratic Party the party of racial tolerance and legal equality.

GOP: SLOGANS AND IMPACTS

Which brings us to racism without hoods.

In a 1991 interview, Lee Atwater reflected on the political arc of racial pandering: "By 1968, you can't say the 'N word'—that hurts you and it backfires. So you say stuff like, 'forced busing,' 'states' rights.' And you're getting so abstract—now you're talking about cutting taxes."

That's a brilliant self-own by the GOP's most successful racial arsonist. It anticipated an era when artful metaphors, euphemisms, and dog whistles were needed to signal that a candidate or party was for White nationalism. Nixon's campaign theme of "Law and Order" seemed ostensibly about crime but, as John Ehrlichman later admitted, the goal was also to make people think "Black" when they heard this phrase and the "War on Drugs."

Same deal when Reagan announced his 1980 presidential campaign in Philadelphia, Mississippi (notorious as the place where three civil rights workers were murdered in 1963), and then ran against a composite, fictitious "welfare queen." In ads, George H. W. Bush exploited a menacing-looking Willie Horton. Horton was a Black man who was paroled by the Democratic nominee, Governor Mike Dukakis, and then went on to rape a white woman. Perennial GOP disparagement of "Big Government" works both as an appeal to shrink government as well as to diminish the most influential institution pushing for minority hiring.

Two more recent codas update Atwater's admission of veiled prejudice. One is "Great Replacement Theory," pushed initially by Tucker Carlson and then recycled by Trump. It claims that the real motive of Democrats who push for immigration from countries with large minority populations is to replace older white Republicans with dark-skinned immigrants as voters and workers. That's a completely fabricated hobgoblin, with the only evidence being the accusation itself . . . yet over half of Republicans agree in polls. (Sorry, but

Hitler said the same thing a century ago about Jews and Aryans.)

Second is "critical race theory" (CRT), also discussed above in in chapter 1 on "Freedom . . . for Whom?" A scholarly term created by the late law professor Derrick Bell, it's a perfectly reasonable construct that traces the effects of systemic racism over time in American institutions. In a review of Robert P. Jones's recent important volume, *The Roots of White Supremacy*, Yale history professor Ned Blackhawk wrote that "a nation cannot fully achieve its ethical and political aspirations while living with falsehoods about its past."

Seems almost self-evident, right? But when presidential candidate Ron DeSantis needed a fresh way to validate his anti-Black bona fides, he got the GOP Florida legislature to enact a law allowing local school boards to ban books and curricula that might make white children feel guilty about what their ancestors did. "We need education, not indoctrination," he solemnly lectured his state and the national media.

If that sounds insane and unconstitutional that's because it *is* insane and unconstitutional. Since when is pure speech banned that *might* make people uncomfortable? The word "Mafia" could offend Italians or a reference to the "Holocaust" could make older German Americans squeamish. To use a phrase in constitutional law, such restrictions would have a "chilling effect" on any book or speech about civil rights.

Indeed, this is precisely the motive behind CRT, according to its chief propagandist, Ehrlichman-imitator Charles Rufo. "The goal is to have the public read something crazy in the newspaper and immediately think 'critical race theory,'" he wrote on Twitter in 2022. Unable to resist further bragging about his secret sauce, he added, "Taking this issue and educating 175 million American adults in a very short period of time, it's an astonishing thing."

Also astonishing was how previously in the late 1970s, when the author was a "moderator" on Bill Buckley's *Firing Line* on PBS, he asked the host and Rich Lowry, editor in chief of the *National Review*—both brilliant white men—if racism was still a big problem in America. They both politely said "no," except for some outliers here and there.

Today it's absurd to deny the impact of systemic racism. Here's the data on Black Americans: they own one-eighth the wealth of whites—and for every dollar earned by a white worker, a Black one earns sixty cents; get six times harsher punishments if convicted of the same crime; receive an average of $2,200 per pupil less in public schools; live in far more polluted communities ("environmental racism") like Flint, Michigan, and Jackson, Mississippi; suffer a death rate three times higher for pregnant Black women and two times greater for infant deaths; have twice the unemployment rate and far worse health outcomes; have been denied home mortgages far more frequently with the same economic profiles as white applicants; and comprise half of all inmates sentenced for nonviolent crimes in mass incarceration.

It's probably time for the two-thirds of Republicans who say in polls that there is discrimination against white people to be asked if they'd trade places with a person of color. Can you guess the response? (Comedian Chris Rock went there: "No white person wants to change places with a Black person. [Not] even me—and I'm rich!")

Only racial apologists pretend that racism has gone the way of spittoons and travel by blimps. If racial discrimination wasn't a cause for all the documented discrimination mentioned, what could have been? After Nikki Haley, herself a minority, said that America has not been a racist country, Whoopi Goldberg couldn't resist: "Black folks didn't climb up trees and lynch themselves." A vanishingly few white scholars blame Black inferiority or the "Black family" (Charles Murray). But the MAGAverse largely sidesteps this discussion since ignoring intergenerational prejudice is a lot easier than ending it.

Recent policy battles confirm who's behind stalling further racial progress:

- ***Alabama: With All Deliberate Delay.***
  Gerrymandering is a practice found nowhere in the Constitution or statutory law that allows state legislatures to draw congressional districts so that, as it's often said, incumbents choose their voters rather than voters choosing their incumbents.

  Gerrymanders that merely grossly favor a party in control of its state legislature are ugly but lawful; however, extreme racial gerrymanders are prohibited under current interpretations of the 1965 Voting Rights Act, as updated. The Trump Supreme Court concluded that five state gerrymanders were racially suspect but also that it was too late in the 2022 cycle to do anything about it—so existing state GOP maps controlled elections in November 2022, which alone enabled Republicans to win their very narrow House majority.

  One was Alabama, where a population that is 27 percent Black produced a lineup with only one out of seven seats held by a non-white representative. But

the Supreme Court ordered the state to redraw the
map so that a second seat would be at least politically
competitive for a Black candidate. The Republican
state legislature, however, simply refused. A three-
member panel of the Court of Appeals was not pleased.
"The law requires the creation of an additional district
that affords Black Alabamans a fair and reasonable
opportunity to elect candidates of their choice. The
2023 plan plainly fails to do so." At the court hearing,
Judge Terry F. Moorer, a Trump appointee, said,
"What I hear you saying is that the state of Alabama
deliberately disregarded our instructions."

Alabama's Confederate strategy has been deliberate
obstruction—from the 1860s to Governor George
Wallace standing "in the schoolhouse door" in 1965
to frustrate court-ordered integration. This modern
version of "nullification" was finally shut down by the
Justices in a Fall 2023 decision, presumably in time for
the 2024 election.

- **_Affirmative Action_**. President Lyndon Johnson came
up with the metaphor that helped to clarify the 1960s
civil rights laws and affirmative action: "You cannot
take a person who, for years, has been hobbled by
chains," he said at a 1965 commencement address, "and
liberate him and bring him up to the starting line of
a race and then say, 'You are free to compete with all
the others' and still justly believe that you have been
completely fair."

But when three Trump appointments joined the
Court, Chief Justice Roberts was able to turn LBJ on

his head by pretending that modern civil rights laws designed to overturn racial oppression were the same thing as laws that were designed to—and did—oppress minorities for centuries,

This Roberts "twistification" (a coinage of Jefferson) is reinforced on every MLK holiday when Republicans, searching for something positive to say about King and race, quote him out of context to stand for the opposite of his life's work. They laud his "dream" that "my four little children will one day live in a nation where they will not be judged by the color of their skin but by the content of their character." That is, he aspired to a day when discrimination by race would disappear, certainly not intending to avoid all talk about racial discrimination while it was still prevalent.

Republicans manage to skip over the "magnificent words" of the Constitution and the Declaration of Independence, said King, as constituting "a promissory note to all men—yes Black men as well as white men—that would guarantee unalienable rights of life, liberty, and the pursuit of happiness. It is obvious today America has defaulted on this promissory note insofar as her citizens of color are concerned."

This doesn't sound like a man whose personal mission was to ignore racial discrimination.

The dueling opinions of Justices Thomas and Jackson in the 2023 case ending affirmative action are also among the most revealing on the role of race in America. In an unusual tone of personal pique, Thomas condemned Jackson's view that "almost all of

life's outcomes may be unhesitatingly ascribed to race
. . . [which is] an insult to individual achievement and
cancerous to young minds seeking to push through
barriers."

Yet Jackson doesn't say or imply that race is the *only*
thing holding people back, but that it is surely "*a*" thing
doing that. Ignoring the legacy of racism, she wrote in
her dissent, is to perpetuate it: "Gulf-sized race-based
gaps exist with respect to the health, wealth, and well-
being of American citizens. They were created in the
distant past, but have indisputably been passed down
to the present day through the generations." Only an
idiot or extremist would question that—and Thomas is
certainly no idiot.*

Before Trump's three High Court nominations, the
Thomas view didn't command a majority; after the
electoral college selected Trump, it did.

- *Police Violence.* True to form, Trump couldn't even
  acknowledge the problem of police violence against
  minorities. When asked in 2019 on CBS why "so many
  Black people are shot by the police?" he answered,
  "There are also a lot of white people shot by the
  police, a lot of white people . . . I can't believe that you

---

* Another flaw in Thomas's thinking is that people may assume that only a
racial preference could explain a person of color at a leading university. While
some white people do conveniently think that (while ignoring the weight of legacy admissions), it didn't bother Sonia Sotomayor and Barack Obama. They have
comfortably acknowledged that such programs no doubt did help their educational
advancement and set the stage for their extraordinary public successes. As a matter of public policy, boosting minority attendance at law and medical schools is
easily worth the price of such grousing.

asked me such a question." (As a percentage of the population, there were three times more Black victims than white.) His response then repeated his affection for Nixon's "Law and Order," an unsubtle effort to associate Blacks and crime.

But the regularity of police violence over the past decade—magnified by the proliferation of police videos—left little to the imagination. Amadou Diallo, Eric Garner, Michael Brown, Breonna Taylor, and Trayvon Martin became household names. They were reminders of the worst racial aspects of American history, of lynch mobs with cheering spectators and the killers of Emmett Till in 1956, smiling as they admitted their guilt to *Look* magazine after being acquitted.

Public anger peaked in May 2020 when police officer Derek Chauvin killed an unarmed suspect, George Floyd, by pressing his knee down on the prone victim's neck for an excruciating eight minutes and forty-five seconds. The dying Floyd repeatedly said "I can't breathe" and called out for his mother. Chauvin was convicted of second-degree murder and is appealing.

After such race-related violence, the two political parties go to their respective corners. With unfailing consistency, Governors Abbott and DeSantis, senators Cruz and Rubio, and Republican leaders in both chambers and in all GOP state legislatures mumbled that talking about guns after gun violence "was the wrong time," offered their "thoughts and prayers" to stricken families and communities, and acted as if the

Second Amendment (as rewritten by Justice Scalia) was the only Amendment.

Democrats, on the other hand, agree that if America could reduce by two-thirds auto deaths and smoking by smart public policies, why was it impotent when a hundred people a day were dying from guns (roughly half homicides, half suicides)? Led by Senator Chris Murphy, they persistently offered ideas that have worked in various states and countries: universal background checks; raising the age to buy assault weapons to twenty-one or twenty-five—or banning entirely the sale of such "weapons of war"; requiring that procurement authorities only purchase "safe guns"; increasing financial penalties on parents who negligently allowed children to access weapons in the home; and imposing a registration system as required for cars, which also can also be used legitimately or lethally.

But this traditional stalemate changed after the video shot by seventeen-year-old Darnella Frazier of Chauvin suffocating Floyd was seen by hundreds of millions around the country and world. It inspired the largest civil rights protests in American history and contributed to a noticeable shift in attitudes about police violence that had begun earlier with the election of Barack Obama and the creation of Black Lives Matter in 2013.

- In 2009, 36 percent of white Americans in a Pew Poll said the country had to do more to ensure equal rights for Black people; by 2017, that number rose to 54 percent of whites, and about 60 percent overall.

- A Monmouth University poll in the summer of 2020 found that 76 percent of Americans—including 71 percent of Caucasians—called racial discrimination "a big problem," a one-fourth rise since 2015; 57 percent added that the anger of Floyd demonstrators was fully justified and the same percentage concluded that police were more likely to mistreat Blacks.
- A *New York Times*/Siena College survey in late 2020 found that 70 percent of moderate voters disapproved of President Trump's handling of the protests and half of self-described conservatives even had a favorable impression of Black Lives Matter. So when Trump the next week said on Fox News that "You don't want to take away our heritage and our history," it likely worked with that viewing audience but landed poorly with the general electorate.

A key takeaway is that Democratic candidates need not be as reflexively timorous about race as were Southern Democrats in the 1970s. They should reframe the issue in two major ways: ask thematically why GOP opponents don't appear to care about equal justice under the law and ask specifically to support the John R. Lewis Voting Rights Act—one bill that Republicans obscenely imply that MLK would today oppose. And as police forces integrate and more Black lawyers ascend to the bench, the law enforcement process will likely continue to tip toward better outcomes.

Lee Atwater would be appalled. Emmett Till's mother would be grateful.

A *UNITED* STATES?

Fact is, not all Republicans are white supremacists, and the party aggressively rejects any such characterization. Yet it's also a fact that most Republicans choose to remain in a party that panders to prejudice in elections and are "silent sentries" (Kipling) in the face of violence and bigotry. Opinion-leaders should help them understand that the strategy of dividing Americans by color and gender is numerically unsustainable in a country growing more multicultural, multiracial, and nonbinary every day.

But progressing toward an ethos of freedom for all requires a political party to (a) abandon traditional zero-sum games that assume that if one race or gender rises, the other must commensurately fall, and (b) create a cross-racial coalition that wins large majorities based on the economic populism that "we're all better off when we're all better off." In his short life, Martin Luther King Jr. was trying to advance such a class-based movement; today, Rev. William Barber Jr. is reviving that cause with his national organizing goal of a "fusion coalition."

Democratic candidates should keep pushing *long-term* for universal programs on climate, housing, child care, prenatal care, taxes, and law enforcement that will disproportionately, but not exclusively, help minorities. At the same time, President Biden will continue to condemn the race-based hate and violence that he has referred to as "the most dangerous threat to our Homeland Security."

The goal is to make not only the "N" word shameful but also the thinking that produced it, even though such bluntness, of course, contradicts GOP grandees who prefer ignoring racism to offending base voters.

Black scholar W. E. B. Du Bois announced in 1900 that the "color line" was the great divide for an America founded on democratic principles. It still was in the year 2000. What an epic tragedy if the Du Bois prophecy holds true throughout the century we are in as well. Monarchy, colonialism, and slavery were thought in their times to be inevitable, until they became impossible.

The best *short-term* strategy to a more tolerant future is to politically stop the party of intolerance in the next election. If they won't respond to moral objections to their enduring racial hostility, perhaps losing more elections by larger margins will get their attention. As for a *long-term* approach, Heather McGhee—former head of Demos and author of the influential book *The Sum of Us: What Racism Costs Everyone and How We Can Prosper Together*—has a valuable wide-angle lens:

Why can't we have nice things in America? The answer is racism. It is the weapon that plutocrats use to divide and conquer. For if we were ever to have a broad multi-racial working- and middle-class solidarity in this country to fight inequality, the billionaires would be on the run. And they know that. That means we have to speak about race and class as inextricably connected.

Here's how I would respond the current political debate over Critical Race Theory. We're a great country, great enough to not be afraid of our own truth and our own history—not Black history but all our histories.' And over 80 percent of Americans believe that we need to teach the best parts of our history and the parts we never ever want to repeat.

Our children need to learn empathy and civics to be great citizens. Yet most Republicans want to defund public schools in order to scare parents away from them. But the enemy is not teachers trying to teach *Beloved* in high school but rather a right-wing cabal that wants to keep us divided from each other. We need to paint a picture of an America where we have each other's backs and can defeat the forces that want to keep us afraid of one another.

INSERT III
EXTREMITIES

Democrats obviously aren't perfect, but they're not nuts.

Contrast FDR, JFK, Clinton, Obama, and Biden with Donald Trump, Jim Jordan, Ted Cruz, Rick Scott, and Marsha Blackburn. In point of fact, we're really dealing with two different species of politicians. One believes in facts, law, and science; the other, not so much.

Here are a few representative comments and actions—out of thousands—that have no Democratic equivalent in the quantity or quality of their extremism or hypocrisy.

- The state of Arizona allows doctors to examine the genitals of children in an effort to detect transgendering.
- The Town of Murfreesboro, Tennessee, has banned public displays of homosexuality.
- After the *Dobbs* decision, several GOP-controlled legislatures enacted laws instituting the death penalty or incarceration for any woman or doctor who engaged in an abortion. (Not easy to be pro-life and pro-execution at the same time.)
- After national security aide Jack Teixeira was arrested in Spring 2023 for leaking classified documents, Marjorie Taylor Greene defended him as "white, male, Christian and anti-war" (while Teixeira is a white male Christian, he also has a large swastika tattooed on his chest).

- Numerous red states are rolling back a century of child labor protections so that fourteen-year-olds can finally return to factory floors.
- Mike Flynn, Trump's first National Security Advisor (for nine days), said in 2023 that he blamed the Jews for being exterminated in World War II because there were "thousands of them and not many guards" and the Jews willingly went along with the Nazis.
- A single parent in Dade County was able to restrict access in the school library to the poem of Amanda Gorman—"The Hill We Climb," read at Biden's Inauguration—due to "indirect hate messages." Turns out that the offended parent had urged people to read the anti-Semitic forgery *The Protocols of the Elders of Zion.* She then apologized, actually saying she has "Jewish friends and is a fan of the series Fauda." (Oy!)
- Two members deserve special mention:
  - Following one school shooting, Senator Marsha Blackburn suggested that one way to reduce such deaths was to arm their grandparents. ("Geezers with Guns"?)
  - Senator J. D. Vance urged AG Merrick Garland to prosecute an op-ed writer for the *Washington Post* for predicting that Trump would likely be a dictator in a second term, which of course is precisely the kind of repression that would happen in a dictatorship.

See, again, John McEnroe in the Introduction.

CHAPTER 6

THE LYIN' KINGS

I can't say that anything that Trump says is true . . . but I trust him.

—Wisconsin voter

Facts do not cease to exist because they are ignored.

—Aldous Huxley

If Trump won't acknowledge his lies and his supporters don't care—then what?

—Anderson Cooper

We're in trouble.

—John Dean

Almost every politician tells fibs, utters white lies, or trims the truth to win an argument—what Mark Twain called "stretchers." But comparing that to what Far-Right leaders say daily is like seeing similarities between elephants and fleas since both are in the animal kingdom. Size matters. We need a better word than mere lies to describe the sustained, will-ful, bad-faith attempts to alter reality by Team Trump, aka, MAGAs.

Jefferson's "twistifications" worked in the day but has obviously not stood the test of time. Or perhaps future generations will refer to "Trumpisms" like past ones condemned "Ponzi Schemes" named after the infamous Italian fraudster. For Trump and his imitators, lies are not occasional escape hatches but their business model. Giving credit where it's due, Trump—who can't spell and never makes any historical references, in part because he doesn't read books ever, by his own admission—has convinced a hard-core third of Americans to accept or ignore his falsehoods. He admitted as much when he told pal Billy Bush that he kept twisting the truth because "look, you just tell them and they believe it. That's it. They just do."

By this standard, it's easy to see how Trump became a MAGAphone of lies. In his only presidential term, according to *Washington Post* fact-checker Glenn Kessler and his team, he totaled a jaw-dropping 34,000-plus lies and falsehoods—up to twenty-two a day in his campaign year 2020. Since almost no one has the time to index and read them all, let's summarize some in three distinct variations: Big Lies/Stupid Lies/Shameless Hypocrisies.

I. Six Big Lies Are the Tentpoles of His Political Life

Birtherism. "Obama was born in Kenya and so was ineligible to become president." The evidence? None . . . though Trump claimed for years that his investigators were getting close or simply asked "where is his long-form birth certificate?" Yet half of all Republicans initially said that they doubted his place of birth. Many still do since, obviously, his Kenyan father knew his baby would someday run for president.

Stolen Election. *"The 2020 election was stolen because of Election Voter Fraud."* To pull off this verbal heist, Trump publicly announced on January 5, 2021 that "the vice-president and I are in total agreement that the VP has the power to act" to refuse certification on January 6 . . . except Pence did *not* agree and saying he did put him in physical danger, according to his worried chief of staff. Indeed, Trump's own attorney general, loyalist William Barr, the prior month "could find no evidence of voting fraud on a scale that could have affected a different outcome in the election."

Nor is presidential election-altering "voter fraud" even feasible when (a) dealing with ten thousand separate jurisdictions counting votes, and (b) the punishment for it is so out of whack to the benefit—risk imprisonment for casting an unlawful ballot or two out of 150 million cast? Why would sane people embrace that risk-reward ratio, especially since a conspiracy with thousands of others would surely leak out?

Fake Media. It's emotionally satisfying to complain about "the lamestream media" out to screw you, which can appear plausible in a world where journalists have occasionally been caught making stuff up but not regularly, much less all the time. Thoughtful people should wonder why the best aspiring journalists still aim to work at the *New York Times* or *Washington Post* if that would ruin their reputations? And what are the odds that only liberal or mainstream platforms are fake, but the favorites of the Far Right aren't? Indeed, why does the *New York Times* have a daily "Correction Box," but not Fox?

Yet, next to "commie," no slander over past decades has had such devastating power with its mere invocation than *"Fake Media."* Not to mention that it relieves its invoker of any obligation to provide supporting evidence.

Vaccine Skepticism. Using anecdotage rather than analysis, many people employ conspiracy theories to explain away bad, complicated news (like a once-in-a-lifetime pandemic taking six million lives worldwide). But when nearly all reputable medical experts say that COVID vaccines work—and the leaders of anti-vax platforms themselves such as Trump, Murdoch, Carlson, and Hannity took it—it's time to be cynical about skepticism.

True, science can get something wrong. "Bloodletting" was an accepted cure in Ancient Egypt and then for centuries more. So perhaps vaccines are the new "bloodletting." (Don't bet your life on it.)

"Biden Is Senile."* Given the incumbent's accomplishments on infrastructure, jobs, drug prices, etc., it's easy to recall Lincoln's classic comment upon hearing that General Ulysses S. Grant was a drunk. If so, the commander-in-chief replied, find out what kind of whiskey he drank so we can send a barrel to the other generals.

---

* *"My Fellow Americans: I'd like to speak to you about memory: First, like everyone whose memory is sharper at forty than fifty, my immediate recall is a shade lower than ten years ago. Hope you'll be fair-minded and weigh that along with my proven experience, judgment, and record. Second involves your memory of what happened when Trump was president. Don't forget his two impeachments, great recession, serial scandals, lethal negligence on COVID . . . as well as his recent four criminal trials and suggestion that Putin invade Europe, risking World War III. Now I may not be objective but hasn't he disqualified himself? So if your choice is down to two old white guys, sorry . . . but then may I humbly ask that you pick progress, not chaos? Thank you."*

With nearly all of the media taking the bait that Biden's too old, it may be useful for surrogates to counter that (a) if the incumbent should die during a second term, there is a constitutional process to install a new one instantaneously (1945, 1963) without changing the balance of power (unlike SCOTUS after Justice Ruth Bader Ginsburg passed); (b) since Mick Jagger's job is the sound of his music, his listeners care more about the lines he sings than the lines on his face . . . and a president's core job is, as Lawrence O'Donnell said, "to make decisions, not speeches"; (c) while Biden has stumbled over words since his boyhood stutter, he towers over TFG when it comes to cognition and smarts; and d) numerically, Biden is four years older but Trump's ninety-one indictments more corrupt.

Democrats can make such logical arguments but probably to little avail since, fundamentally, age is a proxy for people who wouldn't want Biden at any age. As for Biden himself, any time spent talking about it is simply wrestling with a porcupine, except for perhaps occasional mockery along the lines of how Reagan might today handle this same problem—"Moses—funny guy whom I knew pretty well." Or, "Ask yourself, who's in better shape—a president who rides a bike or one who sticks to golf carts?" Or even David Plouffe's gutsy suggestion—to paraphrase: "Yeah, the choice is down to two old white guys. It's now up to you—who's more decent and who's more corrupt?"

The Biden DOJ has been "weaponized" to prosecute and persecute Trump. "Let's be clear about what's happening," said the #2 House GOP leader, Steve Scalise. "Joe Biden is weaponizing his Department of Justice against his political rival. This sham indictment is the continuation of the endless political persecution of Donald Trump." So centuries of the rule of law based on common law and the US Constitution were seminal to democracy . . . until, suddenly in the Trump era, hundreds of grand jurors and prosecutors violated their oaths and conspired to indict him in four separate cases and jurisdictions?

What's pathetic about this last Big Lie is that nearly all GOP presidential candidates in the first 2023 debate felt obligated to agree, which itself sabotages the trust essential for the rule of law to even exist. To repeat: *You. Cannot. Be. Serious!*

II. Those Big, Fat Lies Are Buttressed by Thousands of Lesser, Stupid Ones

These are almost funny if you ignore their cumulative corrosive effect. Space does not permit their inclusion here but prior books and reporters have chronicled them. They include such self-impeaching examples as:

T RUMP: "Friends say I'm the most honest person in the world . . . I'm the least racist person you'll ever meet . . . No one's been tougher on the Russians than me . . . China has total respect for Donald Trump's big brain . . . Obama played golf much more." (Trump played golf 277 times at his properties in one term, eight-fold more often a year than Obama.) On September 11, as Lawrence O'Donnell has repeatedly reported, Trump sought to steal collective grief by claiming that "I lost hundreds of friends in the attack." (It was likely none.)

And of course he changed the direction of a killer hurricane by using a (very) Magic Marker.

---

† Glenn Kessler et al., *Donald Trump and the Assault on Truth: The President's Falsehoods, Misleading Claims and Flat-Out Lies* (2020); Mark Green and Ralph Nader, *Wrecking America: How Trump's Lawbreak and Lies Betray All* (2020).

TRUMPISTS: Now add all those times when acolytes thought it smart to embarrass themselves.

Governor DeSantis said that after only twenty minutes in San Francisco, he saw people "smoking crack and defecating" on the street . . . Fox's Jesse Watters stated in September 2023 that "evidence suggests Joe Biden is personally running the prosecutions." . . . Fox's Bill Hemmer earnestly opined that he visited the town in Europe where "Karl Marx wrote *Mein Kampf*" (oops).

Accumulating his and their falsehoods makes it clear why their whole is greater than the sum of MAGA parts. Only when viewed together do they embody the legal axiom that "to the jaundiced eye all looks yellow" and confirm the wisdom of Sissela Bok, author of the penetrating book *Lying: Moral Choice in Public and Private Life*, "Imagine a society where word and gesture could never be counted on. Questions asked, answers given, information exchanged—all would be worthless."

* * *

Some percentage of Republicans automatically accept all these falsehoods, like cult worshippers of Rev. Jim Jones did. But others need such practiced Trumpian Tricks as the following eight to stay in line. Once readers can spot his BS in real-time, they ideally could become their own Bullshit Detectors:

Cherry-picking—The Black Swan Fallacy

When the data is overwhelmingly against you—say that the polar ice caps are rapidly melting or that 97 percent of scientists agree current trends could lead to ecocide—not a problem. On a cold winter day talk up some unknown study showing that, at one time three thousand years ago, the climate was probably just as hot.

That is, isolate one black swan to imply all are black.

Also, if too many swastikas appear on signs at a rally of folks chanting "the Jews will not replace us," Sean Hannity will reliably announce, "Democrat Bob Byrd was a Klansman!" Which *was* true a hundred years ago when he was in his twenties . . . until he apologized for that lapse while going on to serve for fifty years as a renowned senator. Hey Hannity, one party contains most American white supremacists, and it's not the Democratic Party.

Hyperbolic & Apocalyptic

Newt Gingrich blithely asserts that Democrats believe in abortion after birth—in other words, murder. Do you know such a person? Because the author does not. Chuck Grassley, a Republican senator once third in line to the presidency, wondered whether thousands of new hires to replace severed IRS agents "are going to become a strike force that goes in with AR-15s already loaded ready to shoot some small businessman?" (Unlikely.) When the GOP speaker of the Tennessee House expelled three members because of a "lack of decorum" (they staged a few-minute peaceful protest on gun safety on the House floor), he compared them with the rampaging insurrectionists of January 6, "maybe worse."

But Trump is in a class of his own. He told the NYS AG under oath that he couldn't have participated in financial fraud with his company since, "I was very busy . . . I think you would have a nuclear holocaust if I didn't deal with North Korea, if you want to know the truth." Or as he once acknowledged, the key to this style is "bravado. . . . I play to people's fantasies. People may not always think big themselves, but they get very excited by those who do."

Rhetorical Questions

Few politicians can resist the age-old device of planting a false premise in the form of a question in order to mislead audiences to a wrong conclusion. It's Tucker Carlson saying "why should I not side with Putin?" during his genocidal invasion of Ukraine; Don Jr. asking after January 6 "Do we really want to pretend it's not a false flag?"; and Vivek Ramaswamy wondering aloud if "there were any federal agents on those planes on 9/11?—I'm not saying there were but it's a fair question." (It's also a fair question to wonder what's wrong with him.)

Conspiracy Theories

Richard Hofstadter's classic 1964 essay "The Paranoid Style in American Politics" discussed three habits that appeal to those who need some united field theory to justify their fears: "heated exaggeration, suspiciousness and conspiratorial fantasy." In 2020, Masha Gessen, in *Surviving Autocracy*, explained how "conspiracy theory focuses attention on the hidden, the implied, and the imagined and draws it away from reality in plain view." Social media and AI may now become accelerants of conspiracies.

Consider "The Deep State." It's an ideal phrase to describe something invisible and unprovable in order to become a new "fifth column" for superpatriots. But for disgusting reckless-ness when it comes to spinning a dangerous conspiracy out of whole cloth, you can't go lower than Tucker Carlson comment-ing early in a summer 2023 interview that "I'm not a conspir-acy person at all," just before announcing that Democrats, in order to win, might either assassinate Trump or start a hot war with Russia. (It took a lot to be too right-wing for Fox but Carlson managed to pull it off and was canned.)

Projection

If Democrats criticize Trump for anything, he'll usually simply accuse them of the same thing, despite—or especially—if the truth is 180 degrees the opposite. Hence, Mueller in his report engaged in "treason," House Oversight chair Elijah Cummings was a "racist," and Democrats were engaged in "election inter-ference" due to criminal indictments against Trump for "elec-tion interference." Texas GOP leaders have begun calling doc-tors "human traffickers" when they send women out-of-state for abortions to taint them as being like people who bought and sold children or drugs.

And after all but promising to be a dictator if he won reelection, Trump responded to critics of his anti-democracy program by openly plagiarizing Nazi propagandist Joseph Goebbels: "Accuse the other side of that which you are guilty of." Like this slam at Biden: "The abuses of power that we're currently witnessing at all levels of government will go down as among the most shameful, corrupt and depraved chapters in all of American history. . . . Remember this—Joe Biden is a threat to Democracy." That's one of scores of projections when Trump throws not a dart but a fit.

Insults

MAGA Republicans like Josh Hawley, Marco Rubio, Ted Cruz, and Newt Gingrich are political versions of Don Rickles, though peddling not humor but malice. Gingrich pioneered this brand of campaigning when, as speaker, he openly urged fellow Republicans to use these words whenever describing Democrats: "traitors . . . sick . . . steal . . . pathetic . . . disgrace . . . decay." Little wonder that he now regularly appears on Fox as a wise elder.

By 2024, Trump's insults on his Truth Social were voluminous and vile. One example is sufficient to confirm that he's basically a nasty sociopath—on December 24, 2023, he tweeted at his critics, "AGAIN MERRY CHRISTMAS. MAY YOU ROT IN HELL."

Fear Itself

Humorist Larry Wilmore once joked that Trump was our FDR because "the only thing Trump has is fear itself." At a trivial, though revealing, level, in a decision that Mark Meadows now likely regrets, he went along with Trump's corrupt demands on Insurrection Day because "I was afraid of being yelled at" by his boss. Trump told Bob Woodward in one interview, "Real power is—I don't even want to use the word—fear."

Deny Deny Deny

Author Cliff Sims, in his firsthand memoir *A Team of Vipers*, expressed amazement at how Trump "would deny everything at first and revise as needed—[he] did this regularly." When asked whether he knew anything about Cohen's hush money to Stormy Daniels or whether he was negotiating with Putin's oligarchs to build a Trump Tower Moscow (for which he had *already* cosigned a "letter of intent"), he pled ignorance.

All these categories reflect Trump's and MAGA's keen understanding, as financier J. P. Morgan shrewdly put it, "a person always has two reasons for what he does—a good reason and then the real reason." The *New Yorker*'s Jelani Cobb calls it "implausible deniability." Trump would, for example, pretend to be tracking down Obama's place of birth merely to expose fraud (while reminding everyone that Obama was Black and exotic) and Elon Musk allows anti-Semitic and racist blather on X because he's a noble free-speech absolutist (not—NOT—a far-right troll).

III. HYPOCRISIES

Guns are banned at Mar-a-Lago and all of his properties (despite MAGA assertions that more guns equals less crime). Trump once called Cassidy Hutchinson, a key whistleblower during the Special House Committee hearings into the Insurrection, a "fame hound." Fox's Jeanine Pirro in 2016 fretted that "We cannot have a country led by a president [Hillary] subject to ongoing criminal investigations, potential indictment, and never-ending hearings" yet seven years later dismissed the numerous charges against Trump as "a bunch of theater." Mitt Romney noted that "when President Trump was president, you didn't hear anything from Republicans about how we're spending too much. Quiet as little lambs. Now that Biden is president, oh we're going to shut down the government if we don't rein in spending."

Hypocrisy is not lying per se. But something is off when an entire party leans so heavily on saying contradictory things at different times when only one can be true.

Again, for being a consistently repellent demagogue, nobody comes close to Carlson. In a televised interview, he admitted that "I don't like lying [but] I certainly do it." Despite copping to lying, he actually then went on attack other TV commentators for his sin: "Imagine forcing yourself to tell lies all day about everything [as MSNBC, CBS, ABC, CNN, NBC do] in ways that were so outlandish that people could not believe anything you said and do that every day of your professional life, all your life. Could you do that?"

He could and does.

The Road to Perdition

This volume of deceit by this politician and his party is completely unprecedented. And the scale of those who believe the lies both sad and tragic.

Why Trump does this isn't very complex. Niece Mary Trump, a trained psychologist, thinks that "for him, cheating was a way of life." Whether it's due to his need to get a hit of dopamine, make more money, or sustain his political base, this is his MO, as nearly all memoirists who dealt personally with him have written.

Even before we know the results this November, the cost of Trump's lies has been incalculable. Gun deaths, hate crimes, banned textbooks, altered history, COVID deaths and a declining trust in the major institutions of democracy—Congress, elections, the judicial system, especially the Supreme Court—are all worse. One hundred years ago or even ten years ago, no one would have imagined that one person and movement could have such a profound negative effect on the United States.

So why do GOP leaders and voters so religiously follow him, given all the hidden-in-plain-sight corruption, cruelty, and vanity? The answer for the GOP "leaders" seems simple—they are politicians who aren't eager to be ridiculed and unemployed. "The Emperor's New Clothes" of course is a charming fairy tale but, in Republican circles, it would have required not one truth-telling child but several leading Republicans to care more about their oaths than their ambitions. A few Republican senators in 1974 famously persuaded Nixon to quit, but that was when there was no Fox News ready to destroy infidels.

As for GOP voters, many hate who Trump hates and are happy to hear their private animosities spoken out loud. Others lack enough self-worth to resist riveting themselves to his appearance of "strength." People with small lives and unfulfilled dreams have proven eager to swallow his swagger and exaggerations.

One explanation came from educator Katherine Dykstra, who wrote that "Humans are hard-wired to believe what they are told by other humans who they perceive to be like themselves." Few of us ever encounter someone as willfully devious in our lives and so lack experience for how to respond, except perhaps for well-known categories of acceptable fakers like used car salesmen or poker players.

Yet part of it also involves the darker side of cults. We've seen mass hysteria before, in Salem, Massachusetts, in Germany in the 1930s, in David Koresh's Waco followers, or the phenomenon of when a girl or two faint in class and then many do for no apparent, organic reason. Or when the audience at a Trump rally reacts as one once their guy utters a trigger word (Soros, Pelosi, Hoax, Woke, Let's Go Brandon . . .).

There are two grotesque examples of such willed self-delusion—what physio psychologists call Mini-maxi schizophrenia for when people so lose themselves in others that they lack the ability to think or take responsibility for themselves.

Into the Darkness by Gitta Sereny discusses the case of Franz Stangl, a gas chamber guard who convinced himself that he lacked the intent to kill thousands of Jews because he was "simply doing my duty." Apprehended in Brazil decades later, he was tried and sentenced to life imprisonment in 1970. Then, after years of interviews, he relented. As Sereny wrote, "he said, 'But I was there. So yes,' he said finally, very quietly, 'in reality I share the guilt . . . Because my guilt . . . only now in these talks . . . ' He stopped. Stangl had pronounced the words 'my guilt' but more than the words, the finality of it was in the sagging of his body, and on his face. After more than a minute he started again, a half-hearted attempt, in a dull voice. 'My guilt,' he said, 'is that I am still here. That is my guilt.'" He died of heart failure nineteen hours later—and twenty-six years after the conclusion of World War II—only after admitting to himself that he had wasted his one life on an evil lie.

In the postwar Pacific Theater, numerous Japanese soldiers, believing that their emperor was a god who had ordered them to fight to the death, escaped to hide in the caves of the Philippines and Guam for years after the cessation of hostilities. One was Lt. Hiroo Onoda, who hid for nearly *thirty years* until he was finally coaxed by Japanese officials in 1974 out of his disciplined devotion to hating the United States. (His story is told in a recent film, *Onoda: 10,000 Nights in the Jungle.*)

In ten years, will today's Trumpians be more emotionally able to feel shame at their lack of civic virtue and come to understand the insight of Yale language professor David Bromwich that "the presentation of factual truth matters because we have no substitute world to live in when this world is gone." Or will they shrug it off with "mistakes were made"? Or even keep the faith and look for the next MAGA leader?

   To be continued.

INSERT IV
QUOTES FOR VOTES

- Jared Kushner—"[My father-in-law] doesn't really believe [in Birtherism]. He just knows Republicans are stupid and they'll buy it."
- Fiona Hill—"Not once did I see him do anything to put America First. Not for a single second."
- Marc Racicot, ex-Montana Governor & RNC Chairman—"Donald Trump does not possess the essential qualities of character to lead the nation."
- Steve Levitsky, coauthor of *How Democracies Die*—"The Republican Party is now clearly an authoritarian party. It embraces, condones, accepts and practices political violence."
- Rep. Ken Buck (R. - Col.)—"Everyone who thinks that the election was stolen or talks about the election being stolen is lying to America."
- Rev. Bob Vander Plaats—"The number one hurdle for Donald Trump is I've never met a dad or a mom or a grandpa or grandma who have told me they want their son or daughter or grandchild to grow up to be like him."
- Dick Cheney: "In our nation's history, there has never been an individual who is a greater threat to our Republic than Donald Trump."
- Mark Esper, a Trump Secretary of Defense—"Yes I do regard him as a threat to democracy" because of "when he suggested that we shoot Americans in the street in June 2020."

CHAPTER 7

UNSCIENCE—
Climate and COVID

It's not that global warming is like a world war. It is a world war. And we are losing.

—Bill McKibben

Those in authority must retain the public's trust. The way to do that is to distort nothing, to put the best face on nothing, to try to manipulate no one.
—John Barry, the last lines of his definitive history of the 1918 Pandemic, *The Great Influenza*

America is not only a rich country but a lucky one. Just when we needed a strong leader, a wise leader, and a skilled leader, our democratic republic produced, respectively, a George Washington in 1789, Abraham Lincoln in 1861, and FDR in 1933 and 1941. But luck tends toward the mean and precisely when we needed a capable president to handle the emerging calamity of climate violence and our worst pandemic in a century, the electoral college and James Comey made a reality-TV star the forty-fifth president.

A president needn't be a scientist—indeed we've never elected one. But they should be open-minded, competent, and resilient when true national emergencies strike. That includes being a rational thinker, where facts lead to conclusions rather than conclusions leading to "facts" and being able to act on the best ideas, wherever the source.

There was never a good time for such a bad president as Donald Trump, but his term in 2017–2021—and potentially in 2025–2029—is a tragic mismatch of president and era. For instead of a clear-thinking figure who would pursue solutions regardless of pigmentation or party, we got a sociopathic racist. For that, we are and will be paying a huge price to our national security, economic well-being, and scientific progress. At the extreme, Hitler was a "leader" whose anti-Semitism provoked the flight of Jewish scientists from Germany, which meant that Einstein and others ended up working on the Manhattan Project.

I. CLIMATE VIOLENCE

A clean environment has been a nonpartisan goal since at least President Teddy Roosevelt, a Republican, though so-called "environmentalism" has long faced very formidable opponents. The Fossil Fuels industry has been about the biggest employer and profit center in the country since the late nineteenth century . . . and, as H. L. Mencken said of Standard Oil at that time, it did everything to the Pennsylvania state government "except refine them." And traditional Republican animosity to government regulation made sure that Big Oil since then has had a huge say and sway over our environment.

Something snapped, however, in the early 1970s when the Cuyahoga River caught fire—water usually regarded as a thing to extinguish, not expand, fires. Senator Gaylord Nelson's First Earth Day in 1973 turned into the greatest organized political event ever, with over twenty million engaged in related environmental efforts. And while it did lead to several instrumental environmental laws and the Environmental Protection Agency, signed into law by President Richard Nixon, by the twenty-first century we were losing the fight to slow global warming as a palpable threat to the planet and humanity.

"We live in a world where we are acidifying the oceans," wrote Dahr Jamail in *The End of Ice,* "where there will be few places cold enough to support year-round ice, where all the current coastlines will be underwater, and where droughts, wildfires, floods, storms and extreme weather are already becoming the new normal."

* * *

Real estate developer Donald Trump had respect for land but not the air above it. "The concept of global warming was created by and for the Chinese," he said in 2012, "to make US manufacturing non-competitive." According to *Vox,* between 2011 and 2015, he tweeted about climate skepticism 115 times. Then as president, denialism turned into vaudeville. Speaking of the Democrats' "Green New Deal" he asserted that "I think it is very important for the Democrats to press forward with their Green New Deal. It would be great for the so-called 'Carbon Footprint' to permanently eliminate all Planes, Cars, Cows, Oil, Gas & the Military—even if no other country would do the same. Brilliant!" When touring California after devastating wildfires in late 2018, he announced to an incredulous

Gov. Jerry Brown and Lt. Gov. Gavin Newsom in a near-perfect imitation of Chauncey Gardiner in *Being There* that "I was watching the firemen and they're raking the tumbleweed and the brush and all of this stuff that's growing underneath. If that was raked in the beginning, there'd be nothing to catch fire. It's very interesting."

And he couldn't stop making fun of windmills. "You know, the windmills, boom, boom, boom [mimicking windmill sounds] bing [mimes shooting a gun] that's the end of that one. If the birds don't kill it first. They kill so many birds. You look underneath some of those windmills, it's like a killing field of birds" he told one rally in June 2018. Comedian John Leguizamo thought that "this guy hates windmills worse than Don Quixote. Did a windmill kill his dad or something?"

Funny. But his alternative was what he called "clean coal. I say beautiful, clean coal. And we have more of it than anyone." Except there's really no such thing at scale plus an environmental plan assuming that coal power is clean but windmills aren't is the real joke.

Trump's riffing not unexpectedly led to big and small retreats in the war on climate:

- He pulled the United States, the world's richest emitter of pollution, from the historic Paris Climate Agreement. "I was elected to represent the citizens of Pittsburgh, not Paris";
- On taking office, all federal websites were scrubbed of references to "climate change";
- His administration eliminated eighty-two environmental rules to fight pollution and climate warming;

- Climate-deniers kept repeating that "nature is always changing"—a response as sophisticated as "it is what it is." True, while Nature is Nature, that ignores the past century of industrialization and heat-trapping gases. That is why Bill McKibben was right when he said, "It's not that global warming is like a world war. It *is* a world war. And we are losing";
- The Heritage Foundation's *Project2025* plans for a Trump#47 includes a shrunken EPA unable to regulate carbon emissions from power plants, fewer tax credits for renewable energy, and a bias against electric vehicles. Asked what to do to counter climate change, Diana Furchtgott-Roth, director of the organization's Energy and Climate Center, said, "I really hadn't thought about it in those terms."

It's unclear whether this conservative expert understood the impact of the following facts on conservation:

- The year 2023 was the hottest since records began being kept in the mid-1800s; temperatures warmed ten times faster in the last century than in previous five thousand years because of human activity.
- The Maui wildfire killed 115 people, the most in American history; wildfires in Canada burned thirty-eight million acres, seven times the national average; in California, forty-five million acres were destroyed in the wildfire season of May–October compared to the previous record of 17.5 million acres.

- Louisiana has been losing a football field of land every ninety minutes due to erosion from rising oceans and hurricanes.

* * *

As the world approaches the benchmark of 2°Celsius that may trigger a slow-motion ecocide, there's a fundamental political choice.

On the one side is (a) a fossil fuel industry planning on decades of production of its trillions in buried oil and gas reserves, as well as big contributions to kept politicians; (b) a Supreme Court apparently on the brink of reversing a forty-year-old precedent in the *Chevron* decision,[*] despite Justice Kagan's warning of "the court's appointment of itself as the national decision maker on environmental policy"; and (c) a new Trump administration whose nominee ran on "drill, drill, drill" . . . despite US oil and gas production being at record highs. Its slogan might as well be the title of Adam McKay's movie, *Don't Look Up.*

On the other is a second Biden term on a path to decarbonize the economy via new technology and stronger regulation with the goal of continuing the momentum of the COP28

---

[*] "In its 1984 decision in *Chevron USA v. Natural Resources Defense Council,* the Supreme Court said that when a law is ambiguous, judges should defer to the interpretation of the federal agency applying the law, so long as that interpretation is reasonable." (Greg Stohr and Jennifer A. Dlouhy, "Why a Supreme Court Fishing Boat Case May Be a Game-Changer for Regulations," Bloomberg, January 25, 2024, https://www.bloomberg.com/news/articles/2024-01-25/chevron-doctrine-why-a-supreme-court-case-may-be-a-game-changer-for-regulations?embedded-checkout=true.)

agreement to "transition away" from fossil fuels in a "just, orderly and equitable manner." That requires a very deft approach, coaxing along vulnerable industries and avoiding kickback from working-class voters like the "Yellow Vest" protesters in France.

The challenge is how to counter the widespread prejudice that "to protect the environment, you're going to hurt the economy," according to John Dernbach, professor of environmental law and sustainability. "The air pollution story, based on the Clean Air Act, is a story to the contrary. It's a story where we've had substantial economic growth and improved human quality of life and public health." Only a federal government committed to that message can avoid millions of deaths and climate migrants.

II. COVID

It's not hard to second-guess real-time decisions during an emerging calamity like the COVID Pandemic of 2020. The scientific method of trial-and-error is a life-and-death process involving huge potential numbers. Mistakes are inevitable.

Yet from the Black Death (bubonic plague) that killed off nearly half of Europe in the mid-1300s to the 1918 influenza pandemic that took fifty million lives worldwide—and including our recent experiences with SARS, MERS, Ebola, Bird Flu (H5N1), and AIDS—this country has some precedent to help anticipate and counter similar problems, plus the leading scientific facilities on earth.

So we were not caught entirely flat-footed in January 2020. Presidents George W. Bush and Barack Obama each set up programs that looked ahead to possible pathogens and how to cope with them.[†] It was not inevitable that 1.1 million Americans would die—including 300,000 to 700,000 of them needlessly, according to independent inquiries. Jim Fallows called this, in a definitive deep dive in *The Atlantic*, "the worst public health failure in our history."[*]

Why then has it not yet been an issue in the 2024 national election? The estimated unnecessary deaths of 300,000 to 700,000 Americans—estimates from the Brookings Institution, *The Lancet*, and Trump COVID coordinator Deborah Birx—are extraordinary numbers—300,000 being equal to all American deaths in World War II or the number of domestic murders over a decade; 700,000 is nearly exactly the number of Americans who died in the Civil War. Hillary Clinton suffered enormous political damage when four Americans died in Benghazi while she was secretary of state—not 300,000 but four.

Even before the GOP eventually allows a 9/11 Commission-like probe of what went wrong, a political reckoning is overdue.

---

† The Bush administration created and publicly posted a "National Strategy for Pandemic Influenza" that anticipated a COVID-like virus and how to respond. The Obama administration went even further, in two respects. First, under the leadership of Ron Klain, later to be Biden's first chief of staff, it put together a sixty-nine page, single-spaced document titled "Playbook for Early Response to High Consequence Infectious Disease Threats and Biological Incidents." And it got China's permission to locate a few dozen epidemiologists there to be on the alert for any breakouts or troubling trends. Called PREDICT, Trump refused to appoint anyone or fund it, ending it just as the coronavirus was traveling from China to the United States. And the Bush and Obama reports went unread.

*The best three articles on how the Trump administration failed to respond quickly or well in 2020 include: Fallows, "The Three Weeks that Changed Everything," *The Atlantic,* June 6, 2020; Rucker et al., "34 Days of Pandemic: Inside Trump's Desperate Attempt to Reopen America," *Washington Post,* May 2, 2020; Lipton et al, "He Could Have Seen What Was Coming: Behind Trump's Failure on the Virus," *New York Times,* April 11, 2020.

* * *

President Trump did not do everything wrong: he apparently encouraged or at least allowed "Operation Warp Speed"—a moniker that surely appealed to him—to help finance and distribute anti-COVID vaccines. By the spring of 2021, the federal government and drug industry had collaborated to produce several versions that, though having modest impact on catching the virus, dramatically reduced the mortality rates for those who did.

But on nearly all other measures, Trump flunked his COVID exams.

The earliest anecdotal reports began emerging from Wuhan province in the fall of 2019, despite the Chinese government's aggressive attempt to bury the news. The first confirmed case in the United States was a man who flew from China to Seattle on January 16. No problem, said Trump, the next week. "It's one person coming in from China. We have it under control," lauding cooperation with Xi Jinping. "He is strong, sharp and powerfully focused on leading the counterattack on the Coronavirus."

But on January 29, a dire and widely circulated report from economic advisor Peter Navarro indicated the likely rapid rise around the world and in America, estimating up to 543,000 US deaths and a lost GDP of $6 trillion. Separately, the National Security Council was receiving frightening reports of the spread in China. And Alex Azar, secretary of Health and Human Services, told Trump directly on January 18 and 30 that there would be significant economic disruption and many deaths. The president brushed him aside as "alarmist," adding that "we have it totally under control."

These warnings were conveyed in private. But then Dr. Nancy Messonnier, a leading respiratory disease expert at the Centers for Disease Control and Prevention (CDC), publicly predicted in mid-February that community spread would be likely and that "disruption to everyday life might be severe. It's not so much a question of if this will happen anymore, but rather more a question of exactly when this will happen and how many people in this country will have severe illness." Stocks tumbled. The *Wall Street Journal* later reported that an irate President Donald Trump threatened to fire Messonnier shortly afterward. He stuck to his story that it "would magically disappear . . . was like the flu . . . would go from 15 to near zero."

From early January until he declared COVID a national emergency on March 13, Trump's original state of denial allowed the pathogen to turn into a pandemic. And as with climate change, Panglossian predictions and attempted cover-ups did not erase scientific truths.

- *Figures don't lie, but liars figure.* Trump tried to discourage the Diamond Princess cruise ship from docking in California in late February after a COVID outbreak infected several hundred on board enroute from Japan. He explained, "I didn't want the numbers to go up—I like them where they are." (Fourteen came ashore and went to Ohio for specific treatment.) Same thing with testing. "Please don't test too much" he exclaimed, blaming the rise in cases on more testing.

(Would DWI numbers come down if drunk drivers were not tested for alcohol?) Then, although he knew that COVID was an airborne pathogen, he refused to share that information with the public because "I didn't want to panic people" and because his main focus was on getting the economy back on track, as he later admitted to Bob Woodward. A disgusted Paul Krugman said his "basic position is that thousands of Americans must die for the Dow."

- *Predictions better than facts.* In the face of overfilled emergency rooms and refrigerated trucks filled with corpses, Trump resorted to his proven sleight of hand of treating problems as triumphs and escaping bad news by loudly making good predictions. When testing was slow to start, he assured a White House audience in late April that "testing is not going to be a problem at all. In fact, it's going to be one of the greatest assets we have." (A plan to have thousands of drive-through testing facilities at CVS and Walgreens ended up with several dozen being established.)

We were assured that the number of COVID-related deaths wouldn't be in the thousands, nor 10,000, nor 60,000, nor 100,000 later. . . . Trump eventually realized he was running after an accelerating bus. So he switched in the summer of 2020 to instead repeatedly citing one study concluding that two million Americans could die if nothing—zero—were done to mitigate it, socially distance, or develop and distribute vaccines. *See how much worse it could be!* Talk about setting the bar too low.

- *Personnel is policy.* If FDR had appointed his daughter-in-law the Supreme Allied Commander before June 6 instead of Gen. Eisenhower, it would of course have been regarded as preposterous. Yet #45 allowed son-in-law Jared Kushner—already his go-to guy for trade and the Middle East—to also hold sway over COVID policy. Journalist Elizabeth Spiers, who once worked for him, commented that "Jared Kushner's coronavirus response team is fumbling because it's largely staffed with inexperienced volunteers. Of course it is. It's being run by one."

  Early on, it was widely reported that Kushner had been slow to act since breakouts in blue states were then greater than in Red ones. When New York Governor Andrew Cuomo expressed frustration at the lack of federal help with ventilators, Kushner internally blamed Cuomo "for not yelling enough." During 2020, according to Dr. Deborah Blix, who was then Trump's COVID Response Coordinator, the White House would frequently refuse to issue her reports until she made changes she regarded as political meddling.

- *Fake Science.* Because Dr. Anthony Fauci was getting too much television time with higher ratings than Trump, the president restricted Fauci's TV appearances starting in April as aides Peter Navarro, Lawrence Kudlow, and Kevin Hassett filled in with more happy talk. About that time, Trump and his acolytes—like Fox's Laura Ingraham and Senator Ron Johnson—began pushing an anti-malaria drug hydroxychloroquine and also ivermectin, a horse dewormer. After studies showed that they were both ineffective and dangerous, the Federal Drug Administration (FDA) warned doctors not to use them but not before Trump's public musings mislead some people to try them.

And then of course, in a Task Force proceeding on April 23, Trump infamously wondered out loud whether ingesting bleach could somehow illuminate and defeat the disease . . . this from a candidate who makes fun of Biden's coherence.

- *Scapegoating.* As cases and deaths rose, he was asked if he was in any way responsible. "No, I don't think so at all." Instead, he repeatedly blamed the "China-centric" World Health Organization (and even withdrew American funding from it), the CDC, and the media for his problems. Philip Rucker at the *Washington Post* reported that, in late night calls, "the president was often in a sour mood, complaining about media coverage and carping that he does not get enough credit."

- *Lurching is not policy.* Trump zigzagged depending on the week or day.

  According to Rucker and his team, "One day he called himself a wartime president, with total authority; the next day, he said he was merely President Backup, there to help states as he deems fit. He chose April 12 to reopen the country quickly because he liked the idea of church pews packed with parishioners on Easter Sunday. Then he beat a hasty retreat."

All this now familiar razzle-dazzle showed how, as president, Trump was focused on PR not policy. So instead of educating Trumpers about why the vaccines were as miraculous a cure as Jonas Salk's polio shots, saving thousands of MAGA lives, the Trump administration lost many months in 2020 when, as other countries did, we could have gotten ahead of the curve and minimized the spread. Instead, Trump's disinformation blitz, according to Dr. Peter J. Hotez's book *The Deadly Rise of Anti-Science: A Scientist's Warning,* inflamed the already defiant anti-vaccine movement to bombard scientists such as Dr. Hotez with ugly emails and death threats.

But a modern society cannot prosper when political decisions are made because of pitchforks, not science. Dr. James V. Lawler, an infectious disease expert who advised both the Bush 43 and Obama White Houses, emailed a colleague on March 12, "We are making every misstep leaders initially made [on] table-tops at the outset of pandemic planning in 2006 . . . We have thrown 15 years of institutional learning out the window and are making decisions based on intuition."

Communications expert Jay Rosen at NYU explained on May 4 that "the plan is to have no plan, to let daily deaths between one and three thousand become a normal thing, and then to create mass confusion about who is responsible—by telling the governors they're in charge without doing what only the federal government can do . . . and by 'flooding the zone with shit,' Steve Bannon's phrase for overwhelming the system with disinformation, distractions, and denial."

> *We want a lot from government. We don't want a lot of government.*
> —**John DiIulio**, political science professor,
> University of Pennsylvania

* * *

It won't be easy to bring up memories of saying goodbye to loved ones through hospital windows, but if American citizens don't learn from the failures of our COVID policies, we'll repeat them. The biggest takeaway from 1918, as author John Barry said, is that government had to be honest and transparent to retain the trust of Americans in order to work together in a great public project. But frightened to tell the truth to supporters who regarded vaccines, social distancing, and shutdowns as medical Gulags, Trump lost that trust.

In one sense, the epidemic was like World War II, JFK's assassination, and 9/11 in being an event that everyone knew about and related to. There are now many millions of Americans who know of a family member, friend, coworker, or neighbor who either died from it . . . or needlessly died from it. What could have been a unifying and bipartisan event contained by American planning and know-how became an avoidable catastrophe. His job involved protecting America from danger. He failed.

Could this become an issue that moves voters or will it stay, as Trumpers hope, in the memory hole? A presidential speech and ad campaign could remind voters of this colossal failure: *"America needs to be on the frontier of scientific progress to save lives and jobs. Do you really want to hand government back to the same anti-science politicians who let us down? Why did other countries like New Zealand, South Korea, and Japan reopen their economies and shut down the virus so much better? Why did our country, with 5 percent of the world's population, account for 25 percent of all infections and deaths? Vote for freedom, democracy, and science this fall."*

CHAPTER 8
AN ECONOMY FOR ALL

Only the little people pay taxes.
> —**Leona Helmsley**

If you strike, you're fired!
> —**Senator Tim Scott**

When there's a crash, I hope it's going to be during this next twelve months because I don't want to be Herbert Hoover.
> —**Donald Trump**, January 2024

Some people still insist that theoretically bees are incapable of flight . . . at least until they're stung by one. Also hard to believe was a NBC poll in late 2023 showing that Republicans led Democrats by twenty-one points on which party does better on the economy, the biggest gap since 1991.

How can GOP talking points score when "Bidenomics" has seen twenty straight months of job gains (the most straight since the '60s), unemployment is at a fifty-year low, manufacturing at a thirty-year high, and inflation has fallen by two-thirds?

Have I mentioned that Trump's was the first presidency since Hoover's to end with fewer jobs than when it started?

With 70 percent of Republicans still thinking Biden stole the election, right off there's a huge cohort of voters ready to automatically complain about "Biden's Economy" due to the possessive "Biden's." The GOP disinformation machine keeps churning out disingenuous factoids and adjectives for voters unaccustomed to reading monthly Bureau of Labor Statistics reports. When polls ask people how they're doing economically, most say fine—yet when they are then asked how the economy overall is doing, they say bad because that's what they've been hearing.

At the same time, the media seems programmed to hypothesize about possible bad times rather than report on positive news, or, as explained in news parlance, "We don't cover planes that land." *Yeah, job growth is way up but does that mean a recession is in our future?* Mark Zandi of Moody's Analytics observes that "in my 30 years as a professional economist, I have never seen such recession pessimism."

What's accurate is that there has been a worsening economic outlook—a slowdown in productivity and more economic inequality over decades that have clobbered workers. Economist Robert Kuttner—prolific author and a cofounder of the *American Prospect*—describes the tectonic shift:

> When I was growing up, you could buy a house on one income. People had decent pensions. You could go to college without being burdened by debt before your economic life even began. Big corporations and unions had a sense of reciprocal duty to repay the loyalty of their

workers. Small business was not being gobbled up by big businesses. We once had a kind of compact in this country between the people and between corporations and workers . . .

Kuttner blames the long-term impacts of deregulation, privatization, globalization, the weakened bargaining power of organized labor, and a regressive tax system, all of which dramatically skewed the distribution of wealth and income. Also, the emotional and economic pain of the nation's worst pandemic in over a century traumatized millions of everyday Americans in what's been called "the COVID Hangover."

All help explain why so many—for now—blame the only federal government they have for recent economic distress. Yet that creates an opportunity for Democrats to explain how the GOP's Trickle-Down paradigm is attractive bunk and an Economy-for-All strategy can appeal to more workers like those whose recent strikes led to significant gains.

INFLATION AND JOBS

The public will blame an incumbent party if the economic data are bad (or usually credit them when good) irrespective of events not within their control. To rephrase Donald Rumsfeld, new presidents have to deal with the economy they inherit on Inauguration Day, not the ones they wanted.

Here's the economic hand Team Biden was dealt. In 2020–21, the economy shed twenty-two million jobs; inflation rose from 3 percent to 9 percent, in large part due to rising international oil commodity prices amped up by the Russian invasion of Ukraine; COVID-related supply-chain problems hiked the price of cars and other imports; and consolidations reduced competition in the food sector. The American Economic Liberties Project added that the rise in corporate profits accounted for nearly two-thirds of US inflation. Then once inflation began to rise, there was "some self-perpetuation of it," concluded Jason Furman, chairman of Obama's Council of Economic Advisors.

In response and as expected, the independent Federal Reserve began a series of significant interest rate hikes. But the Biden administration couldn't just wait for a rise in Fed-inspired unemployment to cool off the economy, a cure almost worse than the disease. So it made several big legislative moves to respond to Trump's severe recession. It got Congress to enact a $2.9 trillion COVID Relief Fund that increased the lost purchasing power of families; an "American Rescue Plan" of $1.9 trillion to jump-start job growth; a ten-year Infrastructure Plan of nearly $700 billion to assist aging communities; and an Inflation Reduction Act that began encouraging record investments in clean energy. Also, since some specific monopolistic practices led to specific price-gouging, the Biden economics team began taking dozens of pro-competition steps to lower costs, described in a later section titled *Monopoly—Not a Game*.

Bottom Line: on the one hand, job growth was exceptional as the unemployment rate plunged and 13.4 million more Americans were working. But on the other hand, it has proven daunting to calm consumers recently suffering sticker shock from paying five dollars for a gallon of gas and loaf of bread (as the GOP kept reminding them). And a price-sensitive population of 330 million is larger than 13.4 million newly employed (indeed, the latter number is included in the former).

Summing up, H. Luke Shaefer, professor at the University of Michigan, told a House Committee in late 2021, "This is the best, most successful response to an economic crisis that we've ever mounted, and it is not even close." After a very overcast 2021, Democrats had little reason to be optimistic about the election year forecast for the economy. Yet as of early 2024, they are looking at a mildly sunny summer and fall of 2024. Historically, if an incumbent party enjoys three percent or more growth in the final two quarters before an election, it wins. It was just such steady late growth that enabled incumbents Reagan and Obama to overcome deep economic unpopularity in their respective reelection campaigns.

SPENDING AND DEFICITS

The GOP has been forever flailing away at a piñata with the words "SPEND MORE!" in red lettering on them. In mid-June 2023, *Wall Street Journal* columnist Daniel Henninger dramatically called public spending "The Central Issue of Our Time." He apparently doesn't remember when Vice President Dick Cheney announced that "deficits don't matter" and perhaps is unaware of polling today showing that voters regard that as a second or third tier issue.

This became politically clear when President Biden, at his 2023 State of the Union, teased the seated Republican members for considering cuts to Social Security and Medicare (proposed by Rick Scott, Rand Paul, Mitt Romney, and Jim Jordan). When several began booing and shouting "no," Biden—of course controlling the mic—then cheerfully said that he took that as a pledge that they wouldn't.

All "spending," of course, is not equal. Representatives who force the Pentagon to spend billions more than it even requested to keep a defense plant open in their district are not at all like those who want to invest more on child care subsidies so babies are healthy and moms can go to work. By analogy, it can be fine for a family to go into debt to finance their children's secondary education but not a muscle car for Dad in midlife crisis.

At the same time, Reagan successfully implied that "welfare queens" were responsible for all social welfare programs. This helped make "spending" a four-letter word for decades. In Western European countries, however, where such spending is not associated with people of color, social welfare programs are far more popular and less prone to being easy political targets.

In the United States today, spending funds to fight a devastating opioid epidemic and for a subsidized Affordable Care Act can be popular in rural counties in Kentucky, North Carolina, and Virginia where local hospitals are closing and low-income white families are suffering from high rates of "deaths of despair." Numerically, far more White Americans than Black obtain such benefits. "It's absurd to go after food stamps," concludes Nobel Prize–winning economist Paul Krugman, "even as we offer corporations hundreds of billions in loans and loan guarantees."

Forty years later, Reagan's rhetorical magic is losing steam as a political weapon:

- First, he tripled the debt in his eight years in office; Bush 43 doubled it; and after promising in his campaign and term to eliminate it, Trump increased it by $7.9 trillion to the current $31.4 trillion. "Republicans are for federal spending restraint," argued Rep. Steve Woodrow, "only when Democrats are in the White House."

- Second, much of the total owes to significant tax cuts for the wealthiest Americans under Bush and Trump, payments to save the economy from the pandemic under both Trump and Biden, as well as unpaid-for wars started under Bush 43. (A study out of Brown University pegged the total direct and indirect costs of the wars—including veterans' health and mortgage payments on that debt—at over $6 trillion since September 11.)
- Third, glib comparisons to families going into debt fail since (a) they don't have to spend a fourth of their income for a personal defense department; and (b) they can't print money to escape deficits as the federal government can and now does.
- Nor is it invariably awful to even borrow more than the annual gross domestic product (GDP)—as both presidents #45 and #46 did—*if* the US economy is so strong that all other currencies continue to buy our Treasuries because of international confidence in America's long-term economic prospects. Like now.

Democrats can better appeal to working-class voters they've lost since FDR if they can convincingly connect such investments to specific improvements in their lives, deliverable benefits, and sustained economic growth. Rural counties want nearby hospitals to stay open where they're covered by the Affordable Care Act.

MONOPOLY: Not a Game

Three major merger waves in 1898–1902, 1925–1929, and 1967–1969 led to two-thirds of our manufacturing sector being controlled by oligopolies (shared monopolies). Then came two terms of President Reagan, whose business philosophy boiled down to the popular refrain in the corporate world, "What's good for GM is good for America."

His appointment of corporate lawyers and conservative scholars to the bench—plus a barrage of American Enterprise Institute books and articles finding ways around the original antitrust laws—set the stage for years when policymakers largely ignored the urge to merge. As a result, according to a *New York Times* institutional editorial in 2023, "the U.S. was left with four major airlines, three major cell phone companies and two dominant makers of coffins. A 2018 analysis concluded that concentration had increased in three-quarters of domestic industries, giving companies more power to raise prices, squeeze suppliers and influence policy-makers." A major House report on antitrust and corporate power concluded that "Google, Amazon, Apple and Facebook" wield power akin to that of the robber barons of the nineteenth century. Economist Thomas Phillipon estimated that the US economy was one trillion dollars smaller than if the level of competition in 2000 had just continued.

One recent example: Stacy Mitchell, author of *Big Box Swindle*, described what happened in the food sector when big retailers like Walmart and Kroger were able to squeeze suppliers to hobble smaller competitors. "Five retailers will control about 55 percent of grocery sales," she wrote. "In the absence of rivals, food conglomerates have over time increasingly been able to raise prices and report soaring profits over the past two years . . . [This] led to a decline of independent grocers, which disproportionately served rural small towns and Black and Latino neighborhoods."*

Yet the monopoly problem has gone largely unmentioned in 2024. Why? Two reasons. First, the price paid by individual consumers and small businesses are too individually small—though huge in the aggregate—to power a special-interest lobby trying to change policy. Second, Republicans talk about free enterprise but never discuss the cost of "private socialism" because their largest donors are its beneficiaries.

President Biden, though long known as the "senator from Delaware" for his pro-business tilt, has decided to take on decades of corporate power calling the shots. He used the words "corporate greed" at a union meeting during the UAW strike, and appointed trustbusters like Lina Khan as chair of the Federal Trade Commission (FTC) and Jonathan Kantor head of the Antitrust Division at Justice. Khan's agency sued Amazon in 2023 for allegedly attempting to throttle smaller competitors with its enormous market power. "There's a very real risk," she told the *New Yorker,* that "the economy emerging post-Covid could be even more concentrated than the one leading up to it."

Biden also hired a trio of Sen. Elizabeth Warren's top staff to conduct the most thorough review of federal competition policy since FDR's Temporary National Economic Committee in 1938. The Biden economics team began taking dozens of

---

* "We must especially beware of that small group of selfish men who would clip the wings of the American eagle in order to feather their own nests."—**FDR**

pro-competition steps within their executive authority to lower costs, from getting Congress to allow Medicare to negotiate the price of major pharmaceuticals and persuading airlines, music venues, car rentals, and cable firms to stop imposing "nuisance fees." None were the shock therapy of Paul Volker pursuing 20 percent interest rates but together they added up to many billions of dollars staying in the pockets of average Americans.[†]

INEQUALITY

Extreme inequality in income and wealth is simply incompatible with political democracy. "One person, one vote" is the standard for elections but Elon Musk has a net worth, in effect, three million times the wealth—"votes"—of the average worker at Tesla. This has proven a quiet calamity for middle- and low-income Americans:

---

† *For antitrust nerds:* Tim Wu, author and professor of law at Columbia, was among the Warren-Biden economic intellectuals who helped craft the current policy. In a smart piece, he urged a return to the certainty standard in antitrust law instead of the Chicago School's decades-long grip on courts that favored mergers based on a "consumer welfare standard," balancing whether the benefits outweighed the costs for each merger.

Consider how absurd it would be if the criminal law tried to assess measurable welfare effects in individual cases. Murder needs to be punished without trying to figure out if the particular death might have actually benefited society. When a poor man robs a wealthy man, it is still a crime, even if the defense attorney might show, based on a marginal utility analysis, that the wealth transfer was efficient.

. . . We need to work on improving antitrust doctrines, not turning every case into a welfarist free for all.

Antitrust should offer guidance, deterrence, and rule of law. The various iterations of consumer welfare offer none of these and have instead led to an indefensibly expensive, indeterminate system that has strayed so far from the laws themselves as to raise major questions of democratic legitimacy. The goal of rigor was laudable, but . . . the consumer welfare era is ending.

- CEO-to-worker pay ratio: 1965: 20-to-1; 1978: 30-to-1; 1989: 58-to-1; 1995: 121-to-1; 2020: 351-to-1; now: 399-to-1.
- Michael Rapino, CEO of Live Nation Entertainment, made $139 million in 2022 when the average employee at his firm earned $25,000—a ratio of 5,414 to 1.
- From 1978 to 2021, CEO pay grew by 1,460 percent while the typical worker's pay rose just 18 percent.
- From 1989 to 2019, the top 1 percent of US families increased their share of total national wealth from 27 percent to 34 percent; families in the bottom half dropped from 4 percent to 2 percent.
- Today, 719 American billionaires own four times more wealth ($4.1 trillion) than all 165 million people in the bottom half of the country ($1.1 trillion).

"This explosion in CEO pay relative to the pay of average workers isn't because CEOs have become so much more valuable than before," concludes a wry Robert Reich, the leading chronicler of economic inequality in his books, videos, and tweets.

In sum, these extremes are not the result of some law of economics but rather the tax law. The maximum tax rate on the next dollar of earnings was 90 percent under Eisenhower, 40 percent under Reagan and, because of the Trump tax bill of 2017, now down to 28 percent. In 1961, Americans with the highest incomes paid on average 51.45 percent of their income in federal, state, and local taxes; by 2011, it was 33.2 percent, according to economist Thomas Piketty. Until recently, it was widely accepted that, in the words of Justice Oliver Wendell

Holmes Jr., "taxes are the price we pay for civilization." No more.

"This is a violation of the social contract," argues Senator Elizabeth Warren. "The super-rich benefit from civilization but don't want to pay for it."

It's becoming untenable to laughable for a GOP that claims it is "the party of the working class," when, due to the sway of anti-taxer Grover Norquist, they refuse to agree to any tax increases at all in recent years. So as the wealth of top billionaires has soared since before the pandemic, according to Americans for Tax Justice—Musk from $20 billion to $269 billion and Bezos from $82.9 billion to $163 billion—Republicans continue to refuse to raise their taxes.

Voters are likely nearing or at their breaking point. Will Democrats begin to now have a leg up on taxes . . . or will it take until a 500:1 ratio of CEO-to-line worker or 5,000:1 for all the "Joe the Plumbers" to realize they've been played?

In 2020, a cautious Joe Biden ran on a tax platform that promised not to raise taxes on anyone earning under $400,000 a year. And presumably he won't run on hiking taxes on the superrich in 2024 knowing that the GOP will simply shout "Biden Wants to Raise Taxes," leaving out the part that it would be only for the wealthiest Americans. But should there be a Democratic majority in each chamber by 2025 or 2027, the moral, economic, and political case would likely become convincing to return to earlier tax levels for multimillionaires and billionaires.

Could Musk and Bezos get by with, say, only $50 billion in net wealth? Presumably. And if the Party of Big Business calls that "class warfare," most Americans would likely enlist.

LABOR

The 1935 Wagner Act made it easier for workers to organize and collectively bargain . . . with the result that the five million wage-earners in unions that year rose to fifteen million by 1945. The percentage of workers in unions in both the United States and Canada, a comparable industrialized Western nation, was some 35 percent for both. Today, however, while it's still 25 percent in Canada, it's fallen to around 10 percent in the United States.

> **President Franklin Delano Roosevelt, 1932, State of the Union:** "We have come to a clear realization of the fact that true individual freedom cannot exist without economic security and independence."
>
> **President Dwight David Eisenhower:** "Only a handful of unreconstructed reactionaries harbor the ugly thought of breaking unions. Only a fool would try to deprive working men and women of the right to join the union of their choice."
>
> **President Donald Trump:** "I know the unions. They're dues-sucking people."

What happened was a confluence of factors that kneecapped organized labor in the States: a former GE management spokesman became president in 1980; Reagan then broke the air traffic controllers strike and union in 1981 and, along with conservative guru Milton Freidman, popularized "supply-side economics" as the prevailing economic paradigm—it called for (though didn't achieve) smaller government, lower taxes, and less regulation; and the electoral college graduated two Republican businessmen to the presidency (in 2000 and 2016) who lost the popular vote yet helped create a Supreme Court that today almost invariably sides with management no matter the context. At the same time, America was suffering from the flight of high-paying manufacturing jobs due to competition from low-cost, nonunion labor abroad.

Call 1980 to 2020 the Reagan-Friedman Era—forty years when laissez-faire was king and the public sector (along with organized labor) was regarded as "the problem, not the solution." Ayn Rand's novels captivated many millions of readers more than Studs Terkel's paeans to workers.

Economically, this asymmetry of power meant that by 2020 a third of employers fired workers trying to unionize, half threatened cuts to wages and benefits, and 57 percent warned that they might shutter the plant in question completely. The real-world result was a shrinking middle class as real wages fell, as well as a decline in life expectancy for workers in America without union-covered health insurance, but not for those in, say, New Zealand, France, or the United Kingdom.

Politically, labor unions that had provided Democrats with votes, intel, volunteers, and funds fell victim to an economic version of the first law of thermodynamics—a thing in motion will keep going until it encounters a comparable or greater counterpressure. The GOP–Big Business alliance helped each, as small business, consumers, and the Democratic Party lost clout.

The very big question now is this: has the 2020 election of Scranton Joe Biden—who calls himself the "most pro-union president ever" and personally joined a UAW picket line— possibly begun slowing or reversing the momentum of the prior forty years of economic Darwinism and the past decade of culture wars?

So far, Biden hasn't changed the conversation in three years as much as the Great Communicator did in eight years. But there are tremors of change. In 2023 alone, anti-union CEOs confronted organizing drives at Trader Joe's, Chipotle, and Starbucks—with 350 of those coffee shops voting to unionize. Kaiser Permanente endured the largest strike ever by health care professionals. The threatened walkout by Teamsters of the UPS produced a strong contract for those employees. Actors and writers went out on strike over pay and AI—chanting "hey hey, ho ho, corporate greed's got to go" in rallies around the country—winning contracts deemed impossible months before. And with consumer demand and corporate profits growing as the pandemic slowed, workers found themselves with the leverage to demand higher pay or threaten to change jobs.

By late year, there were 472,000 on strike, up from only 58,200 two years before. "In example after example," wrote Noam Schreiber in the *New York Times*, "executives appear to have been taken aback by unions' new, more aggressive leaders and their success at rallying members of the public." UAW strikers on picket lines certainly didn't sound like Reagan. And the public was apparently watching. A major Gallup Poll in 2023 showed the shift: two-thirds to three-fourths of people surveyed supported the UAW strikers and writers for Hollywood studios; 57 percent agreed that unions benefited companies where workers organized; those who wanted the labor movement to have more power in the future rose from 25 percent in 2009 to 39 percent in 2017 to 43 percent by 2023.

BROTHER, CAN YOU SPARE A PARADIGM?

Had there been a national election on November 3, 2023, when the GOP held that twenty-one-point edge on the economy, it would have been politically disastrous for the party of "It's the Economy, Stupid." But, of course, the vote that matters will occur on November 3, 2024.

Can Democrats close the gap by then between negative public perceptions about the economic plunge of 2020–2021 and growing good economic news now? Can they reverse a steady shift over sixty years of the white working-class vote from D to R? Longer-term, can they begin putting together a cross-racial coalition that binds people together not based on skin-deep considerations of color but on a shared economic view about fairness and growth?

As pollster Geoff Garin smartly observed, "this is what campaigns are for."

Here, Democrats have a very strong case. Since Kennedy, the average GDP growth has been 50 percent higher in Democratic administrations. Employment over the eighteen years of Clinton/Obama/Biden created a net 46.4 million jobs, as compared to a net 1.9 million new jobs in the sixteen years of Bush 41/Bush 43/Trump—those are not typos; to put it in percentages, that's 96.3 percent of all jobs for Democrats and 3.7 percent for Republican Administrations.

Voters have a "yeah, but what have you done for me lately?" chip on their shoulders. Any major shift from *laissez-faire* to an *economy for all*—or what author Michael Kazin called "moral capitalism" to help boost workers in his book *What It Took to Win: A History of the Democratic Party*—will take years and Democratic majorities in both chambers. But Democrats can start in 2024 by stumping for a far higher federal minimum wage (frozen at $7.25 since 2009); taxing billionaires a lot more than their employees to reverse the flow of wealth now going from labor to capital; adequately funding the IRS to go after big cheats; restoring the Child Tax Credit that had cut childhood poverty *by nearly half;* imposing a minimum tax on corporations worldwide; continuing infrastructure investments; enacting labor law reforms that make it far harder for management to obstruct or delay unionization; and perhaps even experimenting with labor representatives on the boards of directors of the largest firms.

While elections rarely turn on economic philosophy, it's now essential that Democrats contrast their values and aims to the GOP's embrace of free market fundamentalism—which for a century has assumed that shoveling more after-tax money to plutocrats is the best way to help low-wage workers. (Much of the world would still be governed by monarchs and colonialists if serfs had been convinced by such a self-serving and self-impeaching analysis.)

Prominent analysts such as Messrs. Krugman, Kuttner, Leonhardt, and Reich—and Ohio senate incumbent Sherrod Brown running for reelection this year on a "Dignity of Work" platform—are now collectively drafting a new paradigm that replaces the "Washington Consensus" (the one that predicted tax cuts would pay for themselves and that pigs could fly—or what George H. W. Bush memorably called "voodoo economics"). It has the promise to buoy an economy with a vast amount of unrealized GDP growth due to years of regressive tax cuts, slashed public investment, greater corporate consolidation, and a "bust the unions" ethos.

While it may not be as dramatic as the New Deal, a new Democratic paradigm and program have the potential to both spur economic growth and reduce an obscene level of economic inequality. Appreciative workers are also voters.

As Team Biden works to turn "Bidenomics" from a sow's ear into a silk purse, Ron Klain, Biden's first chief of staff, is plausibly optimistic: "The good economic news creates a base for him to run on. I don't think you're ever going to persuade Republicans but I think Independents are coming around that the economy is doing better and I think that'll be a self-reinforcing cycle."

Indeed, by late December 2023, major media finally began reporting news that this was a near-record recovery and the leading one in the world. Even Fox had some segments about the 'strong economy,' with hardliners Larry Kudlow and Malcolm Forbes Jr. chiming in. Might that help give permission to other platforms to report what's on their daily computer screens instead of being swallowed up by more anti-Biden agitprop?

INSERT V
WHAT IS FASCISM?

Fascism originated out of the chaos of World War I and the defeats of Italy and Germany. When Mussolini seized power in Italy in 1922, he based it on a word with an Italian origin—*fasces*—which referred to a symbol of power in Ancient Rome showing an ax encased by a bundle of rods.

There is no one template for a system of governance by fascism, which can vary with each country's particular history and culture. Usually, it stems not from an explicit program—as communism and democracy do—but from a charismatic leader wielding power by threats or acts of violence against unpopular groups and opponents, and assuring that wealthy elites stay that way.‡

But based on a synthesis of the leading books on the subject, there are several aspects that characterize countries with a fascistic bent: one-person or one-party dominance; ultranationalism; corporatism; intolerance for unpopular speech; racism/xenophobia; extra-legal violence; politicization of law; and, if there are elections, disqualification of disliked voters.

---

‡ For the best books explaining the rise of authoritarianism in American, see: Masha Gessen, *Surviving Autocracy* (2020); Ruth Ben-Ghiat, *Strongmen* (2020); Sarah Kendzior, *Hiding in Plain Sight* (2020); Jason Stanley, *How Fascism Works;* Bruce Kuklick, *Fascism Comes to America* (2022); David Corn, *American Psychosis* (2022); Madeleine Albright, *Fascism: A Warning* (2018); Timothy Snyder, *On Tyranny* (2017); Kurt Anderson, *FantasyLand* (2018); Robert O. Paxton, *The Anatomy of Fascism* (2004); and Umberto Eco, *How to Spot a Fascist* (1996).

According to scholar Jason Stanley, it boils down to *US versus THEM*. Umberto Eco, an Italian historian who lived through the Mussolini era, famously formulated fourteen traits that help distinguish what leaders are fasc-ish. Let's compare six of his criteria (in a concession to limits of space) to today's MAGA Republicans:

1. **The cult of tradition.** Consider Trump's core slogan "Make America Great Again" (despite slyly never saying when that was) and "originalists" on the Supreme Court (now a majority). The latter insist that all constitutional questions can be answered by speculating what was in the heads of Madison and Jefferson in 1787. Originalism is a thinly veiled attack on modernity that locks America into the views and values of white men (there were no Blacks or women at the Constitutional Convention) based on the selective history of current partisan jurists.

   For example, the opinion that overturned *Roe v. Wade* argues that the word "abortion" is not in the Constitution—true, but neither is "corporation" which now enjoys most constitutional rights; and why assume that it's awful for a country to advance over the course of two centuries when, say, America could still be governed by a distant island?

2. **The rejection of criticism.** Eco asks whether the values of the Enlightenment—reason, evidence, science—are allowed to produce best policies. But dissent in fascist states is regarded as the equivalent

of treason since there's only one true way and only one leader who says, "I alone can fix it."

3. **Fear of differences.** The "us/them" dichotomy has always been a staple of autocracy, whether the "them" are Muslims in India, Blacks and LGBTQ people in America, or, of course, Jews in numerous countries throughout history. GOP language and policies today constantly dehumanize unpopular minorities—notice how often leading Republicans refer to themselves as "real Americans."

4. **Obsession with plots.** From Birtherism, Stop the Steal, the Deep State, QAnon's crusade against pedophilia, or simply the name "George Soros," MAGA Republicans have spread conspiracy theories to explain reality to not-very-deep thinkers. The purpose isn't to win an argument but just to *make* one to keep voters angry.

5. **Pacifism is treason.** For the fascist, "life is permanent warfare," according to Eco. So the right-wing constantly beats the drums of war in order to always increase the defense budget and imply that critics are un-American.

6. **The Cult of Heroism, Violence, and Machismo.** Recall Jimmy Breslin's jape that Mussolini was "a little man in search of a balcony" and compare that to Trump's raucous, rapturous rallies where he valorizes bikers and cops, always resorts to violent language, will never apologize or express regret, and disparages women's equality and nonstandard sexual orientations.

Each of these criteria can be seen in today's Republican Party, which shows no sign of changing its stripes. "There's a specter haunting America in the Trump years," concluded the *New Republic* in 2023 "and it's the specter of fascism."

It was once considered uncouth to call Trump or any politician a liar, a criminal, or a fascist. Waiting until an Americanized authoritarian party—comprised of dozens of indicted leaders, several thousand elected enablers, and millions of devotees—possibly seize national power in 2024 would clearly vindicate warnings about dangerous extremism . . . though, of course, too late.

HOW FASCISM HAPPENS

Bertrand Russell: "First they fascinate the fools and then muzzle the intelligent . . . by emotional excitement on the one hand and then terrorism on the other."

Carl Sagan: "One of the saddest lessons of history is this—we tend to reject any evidence of the bamboozle. It's simply too painful to acknowledge. Once you give a charlatan power over you, you almost never get it back."

CONCLUSION
THE INCHES OF HISTORY

The ground of liberty is to be gained by inches. . . . We must be content to secure what we can get from time to time and eternally press forward for what is yet to get. It takes time to persuade men to do even what is for their own good.
— **Thomas Jefferson**

Patriotism means to stand by the country. It does not mean to stand by the president.
— **Teddy Roosevelt**

The one thing we know for certain is that the presidential result this fall is uncertain.

History is a helpful but not decisive guide since, like finger-prints, no two elections are identical. One corrupt Republican president in 1972 won reelection with 61 percent of the vote and then resigned two years later with only a 24 percent favorable poll rating. Yet a Nixonian successor like Trump hasn't fallen 37 points after his scandals because, in a country now with Fox, right-wing talk-radio, and social media, it's far easier for a loathsome candidate to maintain support with a base I've referred to as his Cult 45.

Serendipity then compounds the uncertainty.

First, consider how history can indeed hinge on inches: anarchist Gavrilo Princip in Sarajevo in 1914 threw away his best shot at the carriage of Archduke Ferdinand of Austria only to get a second opportunity within the hour when the dignitary happened to drive by the saloon where Princip was commiserating with coconspirators; British soldier Henry Tandey on September 28, 1918 came across a wounded and defenseless Lance Corporal Adolf Hitler at the close of a battle near the end of the War and, as he later reported, thought it inhumane to shoot; on February 15, 1933, Giuseppe Zangara attempted to kill president-elect Franklin Roosevelt but instead assassinated Chicago Mayor Anton Cermak when a bystander jostled his shooting arm with her purse; during the Cuban Missile Crisis, Soviet Naval Officer Vasily Arkhipov refused to approve an ordered nuclear strike on US forces when his submarine commander mistakenly thought that war had broken out on the surface; security guard Frank Wills fortuitously spotted a door kept ajar with black tape during the Watergate burglary on June 17, 1972, and called the police; Justice Sandra Day O'Connor, discussing the 5-4 decision in *Bush v. Gore* in her retirement, privately told a close friend of mine, "I may have gotten that one wrong"; and FBI Director James Comey announced that he was reopening the closed probe of Hillary Clinton a few days before the 2016 general election due to the remote possibility that Hillary's aide's husband's laptop might contain new evidence.

The implications for an America without a World War I, Roosevelt's New Deal, a disgraced Nixon, the Bush 43 presidency, or a President Donald Trump—yet with a nuclear exchange between the United States and Soviet Union—is basically the stuff of counterfactual historical novels. Hard to wrap your head around that. And a frightening way to contemplate what could be in store for '24 and beyond.

Second, there's the final week of many campaigns that resemble Winter Olympics Speed Skating. For eight times around the rink, the skaters appear to be strolling. Then in the last lap, there's a frantic sprint when Skater #1, leading the pack, trips and falls, Skaters #2 and #3 elbow each other aside, while Skater #4 slips through to cross the finish line first. Flukes largely determine the order of finish.

Here's what we do know entering the final half-year lap of this presidential race. The two major parties clash over core values—one optimistically pursues "a more perfect union" through elections and laws while the other wants to stop a perceived leftist Armageddon by any means necessary and go back to the future. The model for one nominee is FDR; the other, quite literally, Putin.

Democrats are happy to keep comparing these two very different candidates given the possibility that might increase Democratic turnout and gain ground with non-Trump Republicans and undecided Independents . . . or, at worst, convince some grumpy swing voters to vote for the least bad nominee. The Democratic ticket also hopes that mainstream journalists and editors will report the obvious truth that (a) they wouldn't exist in a dictatorship and (b) one of the two nominees is a sociopathic authoritarian who, for the first time in a century of presidents, doesn't have a dog or personal friends.

* * *

It'll take years for psychiatrists, psychologists, and historians to adequately explain how people who Donald Trump wouldn't deign to sit down for dinner with were either his happy campers or went along with no questions asked. One early effort was *The Dangerous Case of Donald Trump* in 2017 by twenty-seven mental health professionals. Now during his third presidential campaign, it's late but useful to better understand how America nearly fell victim to an inside coup job.

First, confirmation bias is the enemy of truth. Once convinced of an idea or prejudice, millions of casual voters may then be perfectly content to stay in friendly silos and chat rooms where everyone agrees that Democrats are communists and fascists. And then wait for algorithmic outrage to make things worse. Yes we're talking about Fox and the previously mentioned *The Brainwashing of My Dad*, among thousands of other examples.

Second, few people enjoy changing their minds or even bothering to broaden their perspective. At the level of political humor, a placard at a pro-choice rally suggested one reason: "You know you've been brainwashed and lied to because you've been brainwashed and lied to." In a *New Yorker* cartoon of two fish swimming together in the ocean, one earnestly asks the other, "What's water?"

Third, many psychologists increasingly use addiction theory to explain the ardor for Trump. We understand addiction to alcohol, cigarettes, social media, and sex—why not political groupthink? Could that not also provide a hit of dopamine, an extraordinary neurotransmitter of a "feel-good" hormone released when we indulge in a variety of pleasures? There are studies where rodents choose dopamine over survival.

One obvious pleasure for the party of Trump is its embrace of historian Henry Adams's analysis that "Politics . . . has always been the systematic organization of hatreds." If you listen to nearly anything out of the mouths of MAGA leaders, "owning the libs" is a button they, ratlike, can't stop pushing no matter the cost to their political and personal health.

* * *

Can the corporate-owned major media become a deus ex machina exposing #45 late in the campaign? Good luck with that. Recall how President Jimmy Carter assumed that the press would play up Governor Reagan's proven lie in their one 1980 debate denying that he ever said he'd cut Social Security benefits . . . only to learn a career-ending lesson that the media cares far less about truth than "balance." Democrats consequently will have to rely on their own ingenuity to tip the scales. For as the estimable Jon Meacham understood, "The only way to fix the Republican Party is to have it continue to lose. It will be the ballot that convinces Republicans that they have to do something about this flight from reason."

Here are several possible strategies that could advance that goal:

- **Woo blue-collar voters to the blue party.** Working-class non-college-educated white voters went 2-1 for JFK in 1960, yet now favor Trump over Biden by 2-1 in polls, which is a big albatross around the neck of the sitting president. Reducing this disparity closer to 1-1 could be critical but comes with a very high

degree of difficulty. Voters, of course, are free to judge
candidates based primarily on cultural, religious, or
racial markers, or anything else they choose. But with
the GOP agenda favored by only 27 percent in a CNN
poll in late 2023, Democrats need to specifically appeal
to blue-collar voters to rebuild an enduring national
majority.*

On measures of Social Security benefits, job
creation, real income increases, the minimum wage,
and inequality, economic data are not the friends of
Republicans. Add to that the irrefutable fact that
Obama handed Trump a booming economy in 2017
while Trump delivered Biden the worst one since
the Depression. But even that comparison means
persuading a chunk of working folks to care less about
their guns, religion, and the color of other peoples' skins
and more about their own health and wallets.

The political benefit of even a small such shift could
be immense. Author Mike Madrid of the Lincoln Project
put it succinctly: "The party that creates a multi-ethnic

---

* It's hard to win majorities when a party opposes almost everything a majority
of voters believe in. Eighty-five percent of Democrats but only 30 percent of GOP
voters say "government should ensure everyone has health care"; 81 percent of
Democrats versus 26 percent of Republicans believe "protecting environment has
priority over energy development"; nearly 85 percent of Democrats versus 33 percent of Republicans think "gun laws should be stricter"; by 59 percent to a scant 12
percent, Democrats think "abortion should be legal under any circumstances"; 90
percent of Democrats say they're "worried about global warming" versus only 35
percent of the Ostrich Party.

    If the GOP chooses to keep this up, they may end up a permanent minority
party of white antiabortion gun nuts without health insurance.

working class coalition will be the majority party for the next generation."

- **Remind voters about Trump's character and crimes.** There's an expression in Japan that "after six months, no one remembers." Trump is exploiting that sentiment by running a campaign based almost entirely on repeating that—*You never had it so good as when I was president. Democrats are everything they accuse me of.*

  Free speech allows him to say that, but only the rule of law can prove criminality. So while tedious and obvious, Democrats need to spend some part of the 2024 campaign reminding voters of his lifetime of illegality. In a debate with any Trumper, for example, ask: "Would *you* hire a crook to be your accountant? Since you'd feel shame if your daughter or brother ended up a convicted criminal, why vote for one as president? And if you don't believe in trial by jury, what do you suggest as a replacement?"

  So long as the Trump campaign plays up the so-called "Biden crime family," it would be political malfeasance for Democrats not to keep reminding everyone that, after fifty years in public life, its nominee has never been criminally indicted or convicted of anything, while Trump was indicted ninety-one times last summer. 0 versus 91.

- **Remind voters what the MAGAverse intends to do in a second Trump term.** Due to the rhetorical talents of GOP loudmouths and the refusal of most of the mainstream media to call extremism extremism, many

voters are unaware—or have trouble even believing—
what the Party of Trump wants to do not *for* them but
to them.

This book's opening pages paint one scenario. So
have several big pieces of late in *The Atlantic* and the
Washington Post.[†] So obviously would a $100 million
ad buy starting in October that visually conveys the
personal cost to average voters—again and again and
again—if loons like Devin Nunes, Jeffrey Clark, and
Kash Patel came back to help run Trump#47.

- **Freedom of Choice.** The religious Right in this country
  is happy to define all abortion as the killing of babies
  and to impose their religious view on everyone else,
  despite the biological fact that for millennia life has
  largely been considered to begin at birth.

  Politically, voters agree that it's not the business of
  government to tell a woman whether to have a child
  or not, as election results and polls all confirm. This
  particular issue above all must be dramatized in ads
  that memorably convey the real-life stakes, like one that
  aired nationally in 2023 about a ten-year-old girl who
  had been raped and had to risk criminal prosecution
  to travel across state lines with her parents to obtain a
  lawful abortion. Democracy, it must be stressed, is not
  merely about procedural fairness but it also chooses
  people whom we entrust to protect our families,
  neighborhoods, and country.

---

† "If Trump Wins," *The Atlantic,* January/February 2024; Jonathan Swan, "A
Radical Plan for Trump's Second Term," Axios, July 22, 2022; Robert Kagan,
"Would Trump Be a Dictator?" *Washington Post,* Nov. 30, 2023.

- **Two recent books—*States of Neglect* and *Deaths of Despair*—chronicle the startling differences between states in their quality of life.**
  While there are blue cities in red states and red rural areas in blue states, those that went for Biden or Trump in 2020 demonstrate certain unmistakable patterns: states with the ten lowest rates of suicide per a hundred thousand all went for Biden; the most dangerous cities among them based on crime data are all in the old Confederacy—Bessemer, Alabama; Mobile, Alabama; Monroe, Louisiana; Memphis, Tennessee; Birmingham, Alabama; Pine Bluff, Arkansas; Little Rock, Arkansas; and Alexandria, Louisiana. Blue states had far fewer deaths per capital from COVID than red states, especially after the development and distribution of vaccines. Nine of the ten poorest states in America are Republican states. And lower education and income in rural communities have declining life expectancies due to suicide, drug overdoses, alcoholism, shootings, and inadequate health facilities. *Deaths of Despair* concludes that "capitalism is failing blue-collar men" but it's happening undramatically since they are "dying in solitary shame with pills, alcohol or guns unmentioned in death notices."
  While Confederate and rural Republicans are forever complaining about how the big federal government pushes them around, in fact, according to a thorough 2017 AP analysis, "high-tax, traditionally Democratic states (blue), subsidize low-tax, traditionally Republican states (red)—in a big way."

Especially given a new reverse migration of people of color who left Confederate states originally in the great migration of the 1930s through the 1960s—which are making several Southern states politically competitive (Georgia, North Carolina, and Virginia)—white working-class voters should be confronted with this challenge: how many more decades will they insist that their children grow up in places that value a century-old "heritage" of white superiority over the tangible benefits of America's wealth and national governance? Will they be content to keep tolerating a brain drain to states that provide better education, the freedom of choice, and a higher GDP?

Since Trump beat Biden 57-42 percent in 2020 in Rural America, it would be valuable for those voters to know the facts above. Might not reverse decades of cultural resentments . . . but could for some.

- **Talk about a "New Patriotism" based on freedom and democracy.** "We have one party that is all story and no governing," wrote journalist Anand Giridharadas, "and another that is all governing and no story. We have to tell a story to go with what you're doing for people. You have to offer a compelling and galvanizing vision for America."

A good place to start is by renovating "Patriotism." Traditionally it's meant flags, football, free markets, Bibles, individualism, and a bigger-is-better military budget. While a greed-is-good lens might have refracted the ethos of the silent 1950s and now dominate the offices of Charles Koch, it's getting pretty stale.

A big reason: it doesn't describe a world beset by pandemics, local wars, proliferating arms, gross economic inequality, and elected authoritarian corporatists (now in Russia, Hungary, Argentina, Italy, and Denmark). That means heralding freedom and democracy and denouncing bans on books, abortion, and LGBTQ rights. It should include an expanded civic sector of not-for-profits, voter registration drives, required civics classes in high school, and a spirit of community. That ethos was captured by Rep. Eric Swalwell in his grateful testimony about the January 6 Insurrection:

> Because of what Officer Hodges did that day [January 6], I'm still alive. But voters don't have to do what he did—being beaten, hit with bear spray—to be as patriotic as Officer Hodges. They just have to register to vote and show up to vote so we don't have to go through another coup attempt.

- **Articulate the policies for a New Patriotism.** While it's true that most voters don't closely follow the issues in a campaign, some do . . . and some may be enough in a possibly even-money race. Trump's list of actual "accomplishments," by his own measure, is very short—reducing taxes, abortions, and regulations. Biden's tower over that. And looking back, modern life would be very different if there were no Social Security, Medicare, Medicaid, Affordable Care Act, civil rights and labor laws, consumer and environmental agencies, anti-monopoly laws, the Americans with Disabilities Act, the Freedom of Information Act, and existing gun safety laws. All enacted by Democrats over the opposition of most Republicans.

Looking ahead, instead of the crystal ball on this book's opening pages about what a President Trump might say on April 19, 2025, here's what a reelected President Joe Biden could say at his Inaugural Address on January 20, 2025 or next State of the Union, the big assumption being that he helped also carry a Democratic House and Senate, which is after all now just a couple of seats away:

> *My fellow Americans: I asked voters to help me "finish the job" during the past election. And they did! That was no joke! Now, the only way to do that is with a broad coalition of good-faith Democrats, Independents, and Republicans to reject the clouds of hate and look up to a horizon of hope. That means:*
>
> - *enacting the John R. Lewis Voting Rights Act so that voter suppression, extreme gerrymandering, the filibuster, and secret dark money will no longer produce a tyranny of the minority;*
> - *renewing a Voting Rights Act—and creating a system of verifiable universal voter registration—to stop voter suppression that the Supreme Court won't find a way around;*
> - *restoring Roe v. Wade so that women and their doctors privately decide the size of their families, not a group of politicians in the State Capitol;*

- *fixing the Insurrection Act so it wouldn't allow a future president to try—again—to destroy democracy in a lunge for dictatorship;*
- *establishing an indexed federal living wage to ease the toll of inflation and shrink income inequality;*
- *expanding gun safety to save more children from mass murder;*
- *increasing taxes on billionaires and multimillionaires to renew a child credit that had reduced child poverty by half;*
- *passing a Climate Violence Reduction Act to shift more rapidly from fossil fuels to renewable energy in the framework of a "Green New Deal"; and*
- *creating broader, better health care for rural areas to reduce "deaths of despair."*

One election. A choice between two Americas. Either progress for all or going backward to the Fifties, either the 1950s or 1850s.

The great composer Leonard Bernstein, explained how America should not retreat to some discordant past but rather embrace a "Bright, Infinite Future." That can only happen when we remember that in 1789 we began as a UNITED States and came together after 1865 into what was called "THE UNION." In the spirit of Bernstein's optimism, all of us now need to come together—people of all races, religions, regions, creeds, interests, and ambitions—to orchestrate our different instruments into a new Symphony for America for our third century.

Try to change the minds of MAGAs? Probably not because, as Jonathan Swift explained, "You can't reason someone out of a position they didn't reason themselves into." It takes epic myopia for a party to vote to expel George Santos for his stupid lies but not Donald Trump for his big ones. And it requires a "willful suspension of disbelief" for 70 percent of Republicans to believe that the 2020 was stolen in early 2021 *and* for 70 percent to *still* think so after three years of incriminating disclosures from court documents and investigative journalism.

Somehow, a "political correctness" has taken hold where the Far Right can write books with variations of the title *The Democrat Party Hates America* (that's a real one by Mark Levin) but Democrats are told not to make too much fun of Republican gullibility and ignorance—that might upset them even more. So a private, offhand joke about a "basket of deplorables" exposed Hillary Clinton to months of ridicule but Democrats have to treat possible Republican snowflakes with kids' gloves? Because . . . ? It's not as if a consistently livid Trump and MAGAs will be even more hostile to its opposition and, of course, they only vote once.

Based on their in-plain-sight threats, here are three fact-based conclusions for surrogates and supporters to campaign on at the risk of annoying reactionary warriors:

- **You**. If you're considering voting for a presidential candidate who tried to stop over two centuries of the peaceful transfer of power and wants a second shot at it, spewed over 34,000 lies and falsehoods, lost his business license because of systemic fraud in his home state, sexually assaulted dozens of women, intends to imprison political opponents, wants presidents to be immune from criminal law, has a thirst for violence and Putin, wants to

stop your nephew from marrying the man he loves and
runs a party of theocrats that wants to stop your single
niece from having an I.V.F. baby, was rated the "worst
president" ever by an organization of leading presidential
scholars—then the problem may be *you*.

Indeed, if you want the worst president to again run
the greatest country, the author encourages you to
ponder IBM's famous one word slogan—"THINK."

- **The Base.** Millions of "you" comprise the Base, which
is a political black hole with enough gravitational
power to swallow up all Republican voters and
politicians who get anywhere near it. Remember
the Trumper who, when asked on TV what to do
with liberals, placidly replied, "Kill them all." And
remember when Trump during the peak of COVID
admitted that he had taken the vaccine and his
crowd started booing? He looked stunned, changed
the subject, and never repeated that again at a rally.
Ditto McConnell, McCarthy, Cruz, Rubio, Graham,
and many others when they at first criticized #45 for
something only to quickly eat their words when they
heard from infuriated party faithful.

The Base is comprised of evangelical authoritarians,
economic elites, QAnon members who call Democrats
"pedophiles" and the 64 percent who said they'd
support Trump this fall even if he were convicted
of a crime(s). It's as if we're witnessing in real-time
a casting call for the rowdy jury in the 2006 film
Idiocracy—which was supposed to be satire about
America suffering from Darwinism in reverse.

- **Bad Faith.** In a functioning two party democracy, good faith compromises are sine qua nons. So disagreements over the size of the annual budget are normal. Today's GOP, however, are abnormal bad-faith actors. Like those 139 Republican members who cowered while under assault on Jan. 6 yet now call those convicted of attacking them "hostages." Or like Reps. Comer and Jordan repeating hundreds of times on Fox that Biden took a big bribe based on a very credible "FBI source" . . . who ended up arrested and indicted for lying on behalf of Russians who wanted to smear Hunter and Joe. (Apparently being a Trumper caught *red* handed means you never have to say you're sorry.)

One sequence tells the whole story of bad faith. Trump kept shouting that immigrants at the Southern border were "an invasion" killing thousands of children with smuggled Fentanyl. But when Biden and McConnell agreed on a bi-partisan reform to significantly tighten border controls—and Johnson rejected the agreement because they preferred to run on the issue rather than solve it. As for children dying from Fentanyl and Russia conquering Ukraine . . . too bad.

The National Border Guards Council, which endorsed Trump, denounced his abandonment; so did the *Wall Street Journal*. Senator Krysten Sinema, who represents a border state and was part of the unanimous negotiating team, was furious over the betrayal. "My Republican colleagues changed their minds less than twenty-four hours after we released the bill. Turns out they were all talk and no action . . . After all their cable news appearances and campaign photo ops in the desert, this crisis isn't much of a crisis after all."

So unless something changes, Ukraine could lose its essential arms package and perhaps its democratic sovereignty and the border allows terrorists and Fentanyl to keep invading America. These are serious issues but not serious people.

It's one thing to have a Fringe Fourth, as all Western democracies do, that follows demagogues who advocate ultranationalism, hatred of minorities, jingoism, militarism, and oligarchy. But should that number rise to a third or 40 percent of voters, it becomes a dry forest awaiting a spark and wind. What's the precise tipping point? Looks like we'll find out.

> *Trump's extremism is THE story of the 2024 election. Everything else is just window dressing.*
> —**Tom Edsall,** *New York Times*

Like so much in life—from success in war, sports, school, and business—this culminating political struggle may come down to not only "inches" but also personal willfulness. "In every battle," wrote Gen. Ulysses S. Grant, "there comes a time when both sides consider themselves beaten. Then he who continues the attack wins."

Democrats have a majority but, in Grant's sense, do they have the intensity to keep advancing? At the very least, MAGA

leaders show a zeal for combat, if not a win-at-any-cost morality. That will probably only accelerate as Trump believes that
the best or only way to avoid prison is to retake the presidency.

Knowing the stakes, it's now up to Biden-Harris, Democratic
allies, progressive organizations, and a mainstream media pursuing truth to persuade undecided voters what a government
run by Trump, Johnson, and Bannon would look like. One grim
view was laid out by a much-discussed November 30, 2023 article by Robert Kagan in the *Washington Post*: "In a few years
we have gone from being relatively secure in our Democracy to
being a few short steps and a matter of months away from the
possibility of dictatorship."

So will it be America or Trump? Since it can't be both, it's
closing time to call them out and vote them out. This November
will decide not only who will occupy the White House, Senate,
House, and statehouses, but also show who *we* are.

And then will quickly come the next test of our progressive
stamina and patriotism—trying to contain MAGA remnants who
are unlikely to call it quits, with or without "The Orange Jesus,"
as many refer to "him." "Reform," as NJ Supreme Court Justice
Arthur Vanderbilt wrote, "is not for the short-winded."

ENDNOTES

Introduction

3 **"and their families"**: Giselle Ruhiyyih Ewing, "Trump: I won't be a dictator 'except for day one,'" *Politico*, December 5, 2023, https://www.politico.com/news/2023/12/05/trump-dictator-day-one-00130310; Marianne LeVine, "Trump calls political enemies 'vermin,' echoing dictators Hitler, Mussolini," *Washington Post*, November 13, 2023, https://www.washingtonpost.com/politics/2023/11/12/trump-rally-vermin-political-opponents/.

4 **"of his birth"**: "HITLER TAMED BY PRISON; Released on Parole, He Is Expected to Return to Austria," *New York Times*, December 21, 1924, https://timesmachine.nytimes.com/timesmachine/1924/12/21/101629154.pdf?pdf_redirect=true&ip=0.

6 **"the United States"**: "Former top U.S. general: Trump movement is 'major threat to armed forces,'" MSNBC, September 27, 2023, https://www.msnbc.com/all-in/watch/former-top-u-s-general-trump-movement-is-major-threat-to-armed-forces-193936453778.

11 **"the Democratic party"**: David Leonhardt, "Millennials Just Keep Voting," *New York Times*, June 5, 2023, https://www.nytimes.com/2023/06/05/briefing/millennials-voting.html.

15 **"a great king"**: https://www.nationalchurchillmuseum.org/winston-churchills-speeches.html.

Chapter 1

29 **"blood for centuries"**: Faithofourfathers.net, "James Madison," https://www.faithofourfathers.net/madison.html.

38 **"around the country"**: Trudy Ring, "91 Percent of Anti-LGBTQ+ Bills Failed in 2022: Report," *The Advocate*, January 30, 2023, https://www.advocate.com/news/anti-lgbtq-bills-failed-2022.

39 **"at birth (Pew)"**: "More Acceptance but Growing Polarization on LGBTQ Rights: Findings From the 2022 American Values Atlas," Public Religion Research Institute (PRRI), March 23, 2023, https://www.prri.org/research/findings-from-the-2022-american-values-atlas/.

Chapter 2

43 **"George Packer, *The Atlantic*"**: George Packer, "Are We Doomed?" *The Atlantic*, December 6, 2021, https://www.theatlantic.com/magazine/archive/2022/01/imagine-death-american-democracy-trump-insurrection/620841/.

43 **"Marc Elias, Esq."**: Marc Elias, "Republicans Want To Make It Harder to Vote and Easier to Cheat," Democracy Docket, July 18, 2023, https://www.democracydocket.com/opinion/republicans-want-to-make-it-harder-to-vote-and-easier-to-cheat/#:~:text=Unable%20to%20attract%20the%20support,plan%20is%20simple%20and%20dangerous.

43 **"Tom Friedman, *New York Times* columnist"**: Thomas L. Friedman, "China and Russia Are Giving Authoritarianism a Bad Name," *New York Times*, April 18, 2022, https://www.nytimes.com/2022/04/18/opinion/china-russia-putin.html.

44 **"this election cycle"**: "TX AG Paxton Publicly Admits He Used His Office to Help Trump Win," Accountable.us, June 8, 2021, https://accountable.us/tx-ag-paxton-publicly-admits-he-used-his-office-to-help-trump-win/.

44 **"won the state"**: Elizabeth Crisp, "Bemoaning Ohio results, Santorum says 'pure democracies' aren't how to run a country," *The Hill*, November 8, 2023, https://thehill.com/homenews/campaign/4299354-santorum-ohio-results-pure-democracies/.

44 **"run a country"**: Johnny Diaz, "3 Residents of The Villages in Florida Are Accused of Voting Fraud," *New York Times*, December 15, 2021, https://www.nytimes.com/2021/12/15/us/the-villages-voter-fraud-florida.html.

45 **"growing for years"**: Atul Gawande, "Can This Patient Be Saved?" *New York Times*, May 5, 2007, https://www.nytimes.com/2007/05/05/opinion/05gawande.html.

55 **"a protected class"**: Ariane de Vogue and Devan Cole, "Supreme Court limits LGBTQ protections with ruling in favor of Christian web designer," CNN, July 1, 2023 https://www.cnn.com/2023/06/30/politics/supreme-court-303-creative-lgbtq-rights-colorado/index.html.

55 **"not a nut"**: Roger Parloff, "How Supreme Court conservatives can support same-sex marriage—a modest proposal," *Fortune*, April 28, 2015, https://fortune.com/2015/04/28/how-supreme-court-conservatives -could-support-gay-marriage-a-modest-proposal/.

56 **"basis of race"**: Jamelle Bouie, "The John Roberts Two-Step," *New York Times*, July 8, 2023, https://www.nytimes.com/2023/07/08 /opinion/john-roberts-supreme-court-racism.html.

56 **"to be overcome"**: Charles M. Blow, "The Supreme Court Didn't Put Racism on a Leash. It Granted It License," *New York Times*, July 5, 2023, https://www.nytimes.com/2023/07/05/opinion/supreme-court -affirmative-action.html.

57 **"joint checking account"**: Joshua Kaplan, Justin Elliott and Alex Mierjeski, "Clarence Thomas and the Billionaire," ProPublica, April 6, 2023, https://www.propublica.org/article/clarence-thomas-scotus -undisclosed-luxury-travel-gifts-crow; Joshua Kaplan, Justin Elliott and Alex Mierjeski, "Clarence Thomas Secretly Participated in Koch Network Donor Events," ProPublica, September 22, 2023, https: //www.propublica.org/article/clarence-thomas-secretly-attended -koch-brothers-donor-events-scotus.

58 **"Judiciary Committee will"**: "Durbin, Whitehouse Announce Vote To Authorize Subpoenas For Crow, Leo, And Arkley Related To Supreme Court Ethics Reform In Judiciary Committee," Press Release from US Senator Dick Durbin, October 30, 2023, https://www.durbin.senate .gov/newsroom/press-releases/durbin-whitehouse-announce-vote-to -authorize-subpoenas-for-crow-leo-and-arkley-related-to-supreme -court-ethics-reform-in-judiciary-committee.

58 **"Supreme Court—period"**: John Kruzel, "Alito says Congress lacks authority to regulate US Supreme Court, Wall Street Journal reports," Reuters, July 28, 2023, https://www.reuters.com/world/us/alito-says -congress-lacks-authority-regulate-us-supreme-court-wsj-2023 -07-28/.

58 **"answer is: yes"**: Josh Gerstein, "Kagan enters fray over Congress' power to police Supreme Court," *Politico*, August 3, 2023, https: //www.politico.com/news/2023/08/03/kagan-enters-fray-over-congress -power-to-police-supreme-court-00109770.

58 **"being a judge"**: "New Code Of Conduct For Supreme Court | The Daily Show," Youtube, November 16, 2023, https://www.youtube.com/watch ?v=yt2qrPbc7Ic&ab_channel=ComedyCentralAfrica

59 **"prefer the latter"**: Thomas Jefferson, *The Works Volume 5 (Correspondence 1786–1789)* (G. P. Putnam's Sons, 1905).

60 **"called into question"**: Oliver Darcy, "George Stephanopoulos grilled a GOP congressman on the 2020 election. Here's why he said it had to be done," CNN, November 7, 2023, https://www.cnn.com/2023/11/07/media/george-stephanopoulos-scalise-2020-election/index.html.

61 **"happy he's coming"**: Todd Spangler, "Amid CNN Trump Town Hall Backlash, Zaslav Defends Ex-President's Appearance: 'He's the Front-Runner—He Has to Be on Our Network,'" *Variety*, May 5, 2023, https://variety.com/2023/tv/news/cnn-trump-townhall-backlash-david-zaslav-1235604489/.

62 **"not always right"**: Oliver Darcy, Christiane Amanpour voices dissent over Trump town hall, says she had 'very robust exchange' with CNN chief," CNN, May 18, 2023, https://www.cnn.com/2023/05/18/media/christiane-amanpour-trump-town-hall-reliable-sources/index.html.

62 **"watched no TV"**: Michael B. Kelley, "STUDY: Watching Only Fox News Makes You Less Informed than Watching No News At All," *Business Insider*, May 22, 2012, https://www.businessinsider.com/study-watching-fox-news-makes-you-less-informed-than-watching-no-news-at-all-2012-5.

63 **"viewers and voters"**: Jen Senko, *The Brainwashing of My Dad: How the Rise of the Right-Wing Media Changed a Father and Divided Our Nation—And How We Can Fight Back* (Naperville, IL: Sourcebooks, 2021).

66 **"Very Different Direction"**: Tatyana Tandanpolie, "'Has the media not learned anything?': *New York Times* ripped for 'sugarcoating' Trump's 'Nazi talk,'" *Salon*, November 13, 2023, https://www.salon.com/2023/11/13/has-the-media-not-learned-anything-new-york-times-ripped-for-sugarcoating-nazi-talk/.

68 **"by more democracy"**: "Quotes about Libraries and Democracy," Compiled by Nancy Kranich, American Library Association, Spring 2001, https://www.ala.org/ala/ourassociation/governanceb/pastpresidents/nancykranich/cornerstonequotes.htm.

Chapter 3

73 **" Rick Stengel"**: Richard Stengel (@stengel), "Violence is as intrinsic to fascism as free speech is to democracy. These rhetorical nods to violence are done to lay the groundwork for the acceptance of violence in our politics. It is dangerous and should always be condemned by both parties," X (Twitter), September 30, 2023, https://twitter.com/stengel/status/1708102186968727693?s=20.

73 **"President Donald Trump"**: Veronica Stracqualursi, "Trump suggests that supporters may get 'tough' against Democrats," CNN, March 15, 2019, https://www.cnn.com/2019/03/15/politics/trump-breitbart-interview -tough-supporters-democrats-violence/index.html.

73 **"Philip Zelikow, executive director of the 9/11 Commission"**: *NYT* Editorial Board, "America Can Have Democracy or Political Violence. Not Both," *New York Times*, November 3, 2022, https://www.nytimes .com/2022/11/03/opinion/political-violence-extremism.html.

75 **"threatened and harassed"**: Rebecca Beitsch, "Judge cites 'significant and immediate risk' Trump comments pose in Jan. 6 case gag order," *The Hill*, October 17, 2023, https://thehill.com/regulation/court-battles /4260659-judge-cites-significant-immediate-risk-trump-comments -gag-order/.

75 **"single-spaced typewritten pages"**: Eric Lutz, "Trump's Attacks On Judge and Law Clerk Triggers "Hundreds" Of Threats: Report," *Variety*, November 24, 2023, https://www.vanityfair.com/news/2023/11 /donald-trump-threats-judge-clerk-civil-fraud-trial.

76 **"the MAGA catechism"**: "USCP Threat Assessment Cases for 2022," Press Release from the United States Capitol Police, January 17, 2023, https://www.uscp.gov/media-center/press-releases/uscp-threat -assessment-cases-2022.

78 **"power of strength"**: Charlie Savage, Jonathan Swan, and Maggie Haberman, "Why a Second Trump Presidency May Be More Radical Than His First," *New York Times*, December 7, 2023, https://www .nytimes.com/2023/12/04/us/politics/trump-2025-overview.html.

79 **"Seattle, or Minneapolis"**: Susan Heavey, "Trump warns protesters to face 'different scene' at his Oklahoma rally," Reuters, June 19, 2020, https://www.reuters.com/article/idUSKBN23Q2F0/.

79 **"be too nice"**: Brian M. Rosenthal, "Police Criticize Trump for Urging Officers Not to Be 'Too Nice' with Suspects," *New York Times*, July 29, 2017, https://www.nytimes.com/2017/07/29/nyregion/trump-police-too -nice.html.

80 **"committed a sacrilege"**: Jonathan Lemire, "Lafayette Square could decide Trump's legacy—and election," *Denver Post*, June 17, 2020, https: //www.denverpost.com/2020/06/17/trump-legacy-lafayette-square/.

80 **"and legally unsupportable"**: Zolan Kanno-Youngs, "G.O.P. Architects of the Post-9/11 Security Order Object to Trump's Heavy Hand," *New York Times*, June 17, 2020, https://www.nytimes.com/2020/06/17/us/politics /trump-protesters.html.

81   **"stand for Impeachment"**: Charlie May, "Roger Stone predicts a Civil War if Donald Trump is impeached," *Salon*, August 24, 2017, https://www.salon.com/2017/08/24/roger-stone-predicts-a-civil-war-if-donald-trump-is-impeached/.

81   **"stone-cold dead"**: Ron DeSantis (@RonDeSantis), "If someone in the drug cartels is sneaking fentanyl across the border when I'm President, that's going to be the last thing they do. We're going to shoot them stone cold dead," X (Twitter), November 9, 2023, https://x.com/RonDeSantis/status/1722653359314739552?s=20.

81   **"slitting their throats"**: Lauren Sforza, "DeSantis 'stands by' promise to 'slit throats' of federal bureaucrats," *The Hill*, November, 2, 2023, https://thehill.com/homenews/campaign/4289921-ron-desantis-slitting-throats-federal-bureaucrats-stands-by-promise/.

82   **"public service announcement"**: Michael S. Schmidt, Alan Feuer, Maggie Haberman, and Adam Goldman, "Trump Supporters' Violent Rhetoric in His Defense Disturbs Experts," *New York Times*, June 10, 2023, https://www.nytimes.com/2023/06/10/us/politics/trump-supporter-violent-rhetoric.html.

82   **"take it seriously"**: Ibid.

83   **"such a community"**: *NYT* Editorial Board, "How a Faction of the Republican Party Enables Political Violence," *New York Times*, November 26, 2022, https://www.nytimes.com/2022/11/26/opinion/republican-party-extremism.html.

84   **"steal the election"**: Annie Karni and Tim Arango, "Court Releases Video of Paul Pelosi Hammer Attack, Adding Chilling Details," *New York Times*, January 27, 2023, https://www.nytimes.com/2023/01/27/us/politics/paul-pelosi-attack-video.html.

85   **"fix gun laws"**: Brennan Murphy (@brenonade), "Rep. Tim Burchett (R-TN) on school shootings: 'We're not gonna fix it,'" Video on X (Twitter), March 27, 2023, https://twitter.com/brenonade/status/1640512268927418368?s=20.

86   **"for military purposes"**: Jon Schwarz, "Right-Wing Supreme Court Continues Its "Great Fraud" about the Second Amendment," *The Intercept*, June 24, 2022, https://theintercept.com/2022/06/24/supreme-court-gun-second-amendment-bruen/.

87   **"Even the loons"**: Elizabeth Bruenig, "Do We Really Understand the Second Amendment Anymore?" *Washington Post*, November 10, 2017, https://www.washingtonpost.com/outlook/2017/11/10/dd6c994a-c505-11e7-84bc-5e285c7f4512_story.html.

88 **"more mass shootings"**: Susie Neilson, "New research puts the 'good guy with a gun' idea to rest: Loose concealed-carry laws are linked to more firearm homicides," *Business Insider,* July 26, 2020, https://www.businessinsider.com/gun-control-research -concealed-carry-laws-mass-shootings-2020-7.

88 **"all their giving"**: Taylor Giorno, "Gun rights groups set new lobbying spending record in 2021," OpenSecrets, May 16, 2022, https://www.opensecrets.org/news/2022/05/gun-rights-groups-set -new-lobbying-spending-record-in-2021/.

90 **"America-last border policies"**: AJ McDougall, "MTG Says 'States Should Consider Seceding' on 9/11 Attacks Anniversary," *Daily Beast,* September 11, 2023, https://www.thedailybeast.com/marjorie-taylor -greene-suggests-states-consider-seceding-from-the-union-on -anniversary-of-911-attacks.

Chapter 4

95 **"Rep. Jamie Raskin"**: Mike Roe, "Rep. Jamie Raskin Slams 'Deranged' Trump Lawyer's Defense That a Technical Violation of the Constitution Isn't Criminal (Video)," *The Wrap,* August 6, 2023, https://www.the wrap.com/jamie-raskin-slams-trump-lawyer-defense-constitution -violation/.

95 **"Paul Krugman"**: Paul Krugman, "Appeasement Got Us Where We Are," *New York Times,* January 7, 2021, https://www.nytimes .com/2021/01/07/opinion/donald-trump-fascism.html.

98 **"a killer! a killer!"**: "TRANSCRIPT: Mary Trump's interview with ABC News' George Stephanopoulos," ABC News, July 15, 2020, https://abcnews.go.com/Politics/transcript-mary-trumps-interview -abc-news-george-stephanopoulos/story?id=71803869.

99 **"as a settler"**: David Post, "On Donald Trump and the rule of law," *Washington Post,* May 29, 2016, https://www.washingtonpost.com/news /volokh-conspiracy/wp/2016/05/29/on-donald-trump-and-the-rule -of-law/.

99 **"his golf facilities"**: Shane Goldmacher, "Trump Foundation Will Dissolve, Accused of 'Shocking Pattern of Illegality,'" *New York Times,* December 18, 2018, https://www.nytimes.com/2018/12/18/nyregion /ny-ag-underwood-trump-foundation.html?unlocked_article_code=1 .JE0.R3Mm.r4pcj1b0p0RH&smid=url-share.

102 **"above the law"**: *Sun Sentinel* Editorial Board, "Trump and a jury of his peers," *Sun Sentinel,* June 12, 2023, https://www.sun-sentinel .com/2023/06/12/trump-and-a-jury-of-his-peers-letters-to-the -editor/.

109 **"altered the outcome"**: Michael Balsamo, "Disputing Trump, Barr says no widespread election fraud," AP, June 28, 2022, https://apnews.com/article/barr-no-widespread-election-fraud -b1f1488796c9a98c4b1a9061a6c7f49d.

110 **"in his presidency"**: Conor Shaw and Brie Sparkman, "President Trump's staggering record of uncharged crimes," Citizens for Responsibility and Ethics in Washington, September 27, 2022, https: //www.citizensforethics.org/reports-investigations/crew-reports /president-trumps-staggering-record-of-uncharged-crimes.

112 **"from the City"**: Michael Powell and Russ Buettner, "In Matters Big and Small, Crossing Giuliani Had Price," *New York Times*, January 22, 2008, https://www.nytimes.com/2008/01/22/us/politics/22giuliani .html.

113 **"like we do"**: David Lightman and David Goldstein, "Giuliani charges Obama doesn't love America; Democrats fire back," McClatchy DC, June 17, 2015, https://www.mcclatchydc.com/news/politics -government/article24780259.html.

113 **"it to anyone"**: Rob Crilly, Laura Collins, Shawn Cohen, and Ross Ibbetson, "'Trump Is in the Clear': Legal Analyst 'Doubts Additional Charges' From NY DA Following Indictment of CFO Allen Weisselberg on $1.7m Tax Evasion Charges After Three-Year Probe by NY AG That Has Cost Millions," *Daily Mail*, July 1, 2021, https://www.dailymail.co.uk/news/article-9748243/Legal-analyst -doubts-additional-charges-NY-DA-following-indictment-CFO -Allen-Weisselberg.html.

114 **"mob bosses everywhere"**: Peter Wehner, "Depraved, Deranged, and Doing Real Damage," *The Atlantic*, April 5, 2023, https://www .theatlantic.com/ideas/archive/2023/04/trump-mar-a-lago -indictment-speech/673639/.

Chapter 5

117 **"President Lyndon Johnson"**: Bill D. Moyers, "What a Real President Was Like," *Washington Post*, November 13, 1988, https: //www.washingtonpost.com/archive/opinions/1988/11/13/what -a-real-president-was-like/d483c1be-d0da-43b7-bde6-04e10106ff6c/.

117 **"Tucker Carlson"**: Allyson Chiu, "Tucker Carlson says protests are 'definitely not about black lives,' prompting backlash," *Washington Post*, June 9, 2020, https://www.washingtonpost.com/nation/2020/06/09 /fox-black-lives-carlson/.

118 **"a White Supremacist"**: Domenico Montanaro, "Democratic Candidates Call Trump a White Supremacist, a Label Some Say Is 'Too Simple,'" NPR, August 15, 2019, https://www.npr .org/2019/08/15/751215391/democratic-candidates-call-trump-a -white-supremacist-a-label-some-say-is-too-sim.

119 **"heist of the century"**: Rebecca Morin, "'They admitted their guilt': 30 years of Trump's comments about the Central Park Five," *USA Today*, June 19, 2019, https://www.usatoday.com/story/news /politics/2019/06/19/what-trump-has-said-central-park-five /1501321001/.

119 **"about white supremacists"**: Glenn Kessler, "Donald Trump and David Duke: For the record," *Washington Post*, March 1, 2016, https: //www.washingtonpost.com/news/fact-checker/wp/2016/03/01 /donald-trump-and-david-duke-for-the-record/.

120 **"were too stupid"**: Eugene Scott, "Michael Cohen's claims about Trump's racism say more about him than the president," *Washington Post*, February 27, 2019, https://www.washingtonpost.com/politics /2019/02/27/michael-cohens-claims-about-trumps-racism-say-more -about-him-than-president/.

120 **"trait of Blacks"**: Glenn Kessler, "Did Donald Trump really say those things?" *Washington Post*, July 25, 2016, https://www.washingtonpost .com/news/fact-checker/wp/2016/07/25/did-donald-trump-really-say -those-things/.

120 **"low-IQ person"**: Mariam Khan, "Trump calls Waters 'extraordinarily low IQ person' in wake of restaurant controversy," ABC News, June 25, 2018, https://abcnews.go.com/Politics/trump-calls-waters-extremely -low-iq-person-wake/story?id=56140886.

120 **"places like Norway"**: Eli Watkins and Abby Phillip, "Trump decries immigrants from 'shithole countries' coming to US," CNN, January 12, 2018, https://www.cnn.com/2018/01/11/politics/immigrants-shithole -countries-trump/index.html.

120 **"George Wallace was"**: "Trump Is Racist, Half Of U.S. Voters Say, Quinnipiac University National Poll Finds; But Voters Say Almost 2-1 Don't Impeach President," Quinnipiac University Poll, July 30, 2019, https://poll.qu.edu/Poll-Release-Legacy?releaseid=3636; Harry Enten, "More voters think Donald Trump is a racist than thought George Wallace was in 1968," CNN, July 31, 2019, https://www.cnn .com/2019/07/31/politics/poll-trump-racist/index.html.

121 **"30 percent college educated"**: Kai Elwood-Dieu, Jessica Piper, and Beatrice Jin, "Elections 2022: The educational divide that helps explain the midterms," *Politico*, November 17, 2022, https://www.politico.com /interactives/2022/midterm-election-house-districts-by-education/.

122 **"about cutting taxes"**: Rick Perlstein, "Exclusive: Lee Atwater's Infamous 1981 Interview on the Southern Strategy," *The Nation*, November 13, 2012, https://www.thenation.com/article/archive/exclusive-lee-atwaters-infamous-1981-interview-southern-strategy/.

123 **"about its past"**: Ned Blackhawk, "Tracing the Origins of American Racism as a Path to Healing,"*New York Times*, September 5, 2023, https://www.nytimes.com/2023/09/05/books/review/the-hidden-roots-of-white-supremacy-robert-p-jones.html.

123 **"the national media"**: Hannah Demissie and Will McDuffie, "Republican debate highlights and analysis: Fiery faceoff on Trump, Ukraine and more," ABC News, August 24, 2023, https://abcnews.go.com/Politics/live-updates/republican-debate-primary/desantis-we-need-education-not-indoctrination-102520197?id=102507215.

123 **"Twitter in 2022"**: Christopher F. Rufo (@realchrisrufo), "The goal is to have the public read something crazy in the newspaper and immediately think "critical race theory." We have decodified the term and will recodify it to annex the entire range of cultural constructions that are unpopular with Americans," X (Twitter), March 15, 2021, https://twitter.com/realchrisrufo/status/1371541044592996352?lang=en.

124 **"an astonishing thing"**: Trip Gabriel, "He Fuels the Right's Cultural Fires (and Spreads Them to Florida)," *New York Times*, April 24, 2022, https://www.nytimes.com/2022/04/24/us/politics/christopher-rufo-crt-lgbtq-florida.html.

126 **"fails to do so"**: Kim Chandler, "Judges reject Alabama's congressional lines, will draw new districts to increase Black voting power," AP, September 5, 2023, https://apnews.com/article/alabama-redistricting-ruling-black-population-affd7b662f65b0b28da42fb88f72207e.

126 **"disregarded our instructions"**: Emily Cochrane, "Federal Court Again Strikes Down Alabama's Congressional Map," *New York Times*, September 5, 2023, https://www.nytimes.com/2023/09/05/us/politics/alabama-congressional-map.html.

126 **"been completely fair"**: Lyndon B. Johnson, "Commencement Address at Howard University: 'To Fulfill These Rights,'" The American Presidency Project, June 4, 1965, https://www.presidency.ucsb.edu/documents/commencement-address-howard-university-fulfill-these-rights#:~:text=You%20do%20not%20take%20a,open%20the%20gates%20of%20opportunity.

127 **"citizens of color are concerned"**: "Dr. Martin Luther King Jr. and the Promises of the American Revolution," Museum of the American Revolution, https://www.amrevmuseum.org/dr-martin-luther-king -jr-and-the-promises-of-the-american-revolution#:-:text=This%20 note%20was%20a%20promise,citizens%20of%20color%20are%20 concerned.

128 **"push through barriers"**: Abbie VanSickle, "In Affirmative Action Ruling, Black Justices Take Aim at Each Other," *New York Times*, June 29, 2023, https://www.nytimes.com/2023/06/29/us/politics /black-justices-affirmative-action-thomas-jackson.html.

128 **"through the generations"**: Ibid.

129 **"victims than white"**: Grace Segers, "Asked why Black Americans are killed by police, Trump responds, 'So are White people,'" CBS News, July 15, 2020, https://www.cbsnews.com/news/trump-black -americans-killed-police-so-are-white-people/.

130 **"60 percent overall"**: "Blacks Upbeat about Black Progress, Prospects," Pew Research Center, January 12, 2010, https://www .pewresearch.org/social-trends/2010/01/12/blacks-upbeat-about black-progress-prospects/.

131 **"to mistreat Blacks"**: "Race relations play major role in political divide," Monmouth University Poll, June 28, 2023, https://www.monmouth .edu/polling-institute/reports/monmouthpoll_us_062823/.

131 **"and our history"**: Maggie Haberman and Jonathan Martin, "With Tweets, Videos and Rhetoric, Trump Pushes Anew to Divide Americans by Race," *New York Times*, June 23, 2020, https://www .nytimes.com/2020/06/23/us/politics/trump-race-racism-protests .html.

Chapter 6

139 **"power to act"**: Brooke Singman, "Trump says he, Pence in 'total agreement' VP has 'power' to block certification of 'illegal' election," Fox News, January 5, 2021, https://www.foxnews.com/politics/trump -says-he-pence-in-total-agreement-vp-has-power-to-block-certification -of-illegal-election.

139 **"outcome in the election"**: "Barr: No evidence of fraud that'd change election outcome," *Politico,* December 1, 2020, https://www.politico .com/news/2020/12/01/barr-no-evidence-of-fraud-election -outcome-441832.

141 **"persecution of Donald Trump"**: Luke Broadwater, "House Republicans Rally Behind Trump, Seeking to Discredit Indictment,"

New York Times, June 9, 2023, https://www.nytimes.com/2023/06/09/us/politics/republicans-trump-indictment.html.

143 **"running the prosecutions":** Fox News Staff, "JESSE WATTERS: Evidence suggests Joe Biden is personally running the prosecutions of Donald Trump," Fox News, August 28, 2023, https://www.foxnews.com/media/jesse-watters-evidence-suggests-joe-biden-personally-running-prosecutions-donald-trump.

143 ***"Mein Kampf"* (oops)":** Elyse Wanshel, "Memo To Fox News Anchor Bill Hemmer: Karl Marx Didn't Write 'Mein Kampf,'" *HuffPost*, August 10, 2021, https://www.huffpost.com/entry/bill-hemmer-karl-marx-mein-kampf_n_611295e8e4b03358451a10c8.

144 **"some small businessman":** Philip Bump, "From GOP chair to militias, the right issues baseless warnings about armed IRS thugs," *Washington Post*, August 11, 2022, https://www.washingtonpost.com/politics/2022/08/11/republicans-irs/.

145 **"those who do":** Reena Flores, "Donald Trump: Living by 'Art of the Deal' as campaign playbook," CBS News, April 1, 2016, https://www.cbsnews.com/news/how-donald-trump-is-using-the-art-of-the-deal-as-a-campaign-playbook/.

145 **"side with Putin":** Timothy Bella, "Tucker Carlson, downplaying Russia-Ukraine conflict, urges Americans to ask, 'Why do I hate Putin?'" *Washington Post*, February 23, 2022, https://www.washingtonpost.com/media/2022/02/23/tucker-carlson-putin-russia-ukraine/.

145 **"a fair question":** Katherine Koretski and Alex Tabet, "Vivek Ramaswamy is turning to new talking points—conspiracy theories," BNC News, December 21, 2023, https://www.nbcnews.com/politics/2024-election/vivek-ramaswamy-turning-new-talking-points-conspiracy-theories-rcna130187.

145 **"and conspiratorial fantasy":** Richard Hofstadter, "The Paranoid Style in American Politics Adjust," *Harper's Magazine*, November 1964, https://harpers.org/archive/1964/11/the-paranoid-style-in-american-politics/.

147 **"the word—fear":** Patrick Boucheron, "'Real power is fear': what Machiavelli tells us about Trump in 2020," *The Guardian*, February 8, 2020, https://www.theguardian.com/us-news/2020/feb/08/real-power-is-fear-donald-trump-machiavelli-boucheron.

148 **"the real reason":** J. P. Morgan, "Forbes Quotes: Thoughts On The Business Of Life," https://www.forbes.com/quotes/4622/.

148 **"implausible deniability":** Jelani Cobb, "From Charleston to Pittsburgh, an Arc of Premeditated American Tragedy," *New Yorker*,

November 1, 2018, https://www.newyorker.com/news/dispatch/from
-charleston-to-pittsburgh-an-arc-of-premeditated-american-tragedy.

148 **"bunch of theater"**: Andi Ortiz, "Jeanine Pirro Rants About How
US Can't Be 'Led by a President Subject to Ongoing Criminal
Investigations'—Back in 2016 (Video)," *The Wrap*, August 30, 2023,
https://www.thewrap.com/jeanine-pirro-rant-president-cant-be
-under-investigation/

148 **"rein in spending"**: Igor Bobic, "Mitt Romney Blasts GOP
Hypocrisy On Spending As Government Shutdown Threat Looms,"
HuffPost, August 29, 2023, https://www.huffpost.com/entry/mitt
-romney-gop-shutdown_n_64ee4649e4b0d1725214940c.

149 **"certainly do it"**: Maroosha Muzaffar, "Tucker Carlson admits he
lies on his show: 'I really try not to . . . [but] I certainly do,'" *The
Independent*, September 15, 2021, https://www.independent.co.uk
/news/world/americas/tucker-carlson-fox-news-dave-rubin-b1919738
.html.

149 **"way of life"**: Maggie Haberman and Alan Fire, "Mary Trump's Book
Accuses the President of Embracing 'Cheating as a Way of Life,'"
New York Times, July 7, 2020, https://www.nytimes.com/2020/07/07
/us/politics/mary-trump-book.html.

Chapter 7

155 **"Bill McKibben"**: Bill McKibben, "A World at War," *New Republic*,
August 15, 2016, https://newrepublic.com/article/135684/declare-war
-climate-change-mobilize-wwii.

155 **"*The Great Influenza*"**: John M. Barry, *The Great Influenza: The
Story of the Deadliest Pandemic in History* (New York: Penguin Books,
2021).

157 **"the new normal"**: Dahr Jamail, *The End of Ice: Bearing Witness and
Finding Meaning in the Path of Climate Disruption* (New York: The
New Press, 2019).

157 **"manufacturing non-competitive"**: Donald Trump (@realDonald
Trump), "The concept of global warming was created by and for the
Chinese in order to make U.S. manufacturing non-competitive," X
(Twitter), November 6, 2012, https://twitter.com/realDonaldTrump
/status/265895292191248385.

157 **"the same. Brilliant"**: Donald J. Trump (@realDonaldTrump), "I
think it is very important for the Democrats to press forward with
their Green New Deal. It would be great for the so-called "Carbon
Footprint" to permanently eliminate all Planes, Cars, Cows, Oil,

Gas & the Military—even if no other country would do the same. Brilliant!" X (Twitter), February 9, 2019, https://twitter.com /realDonaldTrump/status/1094375749279248385.

158 **"field of birds"**: Philip Bump, "Allow us to translate Trump's odd comments on coal and energy," *Washington Post*, August 20, 2018, https://www.washingtonpost.com/news/politics/wp/2018/08/20 /allow-us-to-translate-trumps-odd-comments-on-coal-and-energy/.

158 **"dad or something"**: John Leguizamo (@JohnLeguizamo), "Trump has been saying windmills don't work because the wind doesn't blow all the time. Now he says the noise they make causes cancer. Man, this guy hates windmills worse than Don Quixote. Did a windmill kill his dad or something?," X (Twitter), April 4, 2019, https://twitter.com /JohnLeguizamo/status/1113905479951048704.

158 **"Pittsburgh, not Paris"**: "Statement by President Trump on the Paris Climate Accord," White House Archives, June 1, 2017, https: //trumpwhitehouse.archives.gov/briefings-statements/statement -president-trump-paris-climate-accord/#:-:text=I%20was%20 elected%20to%20represent,will%20soon%20be%20under%20 renegotiation.

159 **"in those terms"**: Lisa Friedman, "A Republican 2024 Climate Strategy: More Drilling, Less Clean Energy," *New York Times*, August 4, 2023, https://www.nytimes.com/2023/08/04/climate/republicans-climate -project2025.html.

160 **"on environmental policy"**: Amy Howe, "Supreme Court curtails Clean Water Act," SCOTUSblog, May 25, 2023, https://www.scotus blog.com/2023/05/supreme-court-curtails-clean-water-act/.

161 **"and public health"**: Rachel DuRose, "How America solved its first air pollution crisis—and why solving the next one will be harder," *Vox*, June 22, 2023, https://www.vox.com/future-perfect/23757949 /air-pollution-history-progress-clean-air-act-environmental -protection-agency-wildfires-smoke-smog.

162 **"in our history"**: Jim Fallows, "The Three Weeks that Changed Everything," *The Atlantic*, June 6, 2020, https://www.theatlantic .com/politics/archive/2020/06/how-white-house-coronavirus -response-went-wrong/613591/.

163 **"with Xi Jinping"**: Matthew J. Belvedere, "Trump says he trusts China's Xi on coronavirus and the US has it 'totally under control,'" CNBC, January 22, 2020, https://www.cnbc.com/2020/01/22/trump -on-coronavirus-from-china-we-have-it-totally-under-control.html.

163 **"on the Coronavirus"**: Donald Trump (@realDonaldTrump), "Just had a long and very good conversation by phone with President Xi of China.

He is strong, sharp and powerfully focused on leading the counterattack on the Coronavirus. He feels they are doing very well, even building hospitals in a matter of only days. Nothing is easy, but . . ." X (Twitter), February 7, 2020, https://twitter.com/realDonaldTrump/status/1225728755248828416?ref _src=twsrc%5Etfw%7Ctwcamp%5Etweetembed%7C twterm%5E1225728755248828416%7Ctwgr%5E39d11f44b78056011a 941a8fde5f0c2794331ae9%7Ctwcon%5Es1_&ref_url=https %3A%2F%2Fwww.washingtonpost.com%2Fpolitics%2F2020%2F04 %2F23%2F12-trumps-worst-coronavirus-contradictions%2F.

164 **"have severe illness"**: Centers for Disease Control and Prevention, "Transcript for the CDC Telebriefing Update on COVID-19," February 26, 2020, https://stacks.cdc.gov/pdfjs/web/viewer.html?file=https: //stacks.cdc.gov/view/cdc/85310/cdc_85310_DS1.pdf.

166 **"run by one"**: Elizabeth Spiers, "I worked for Jared Kushner. Of course he says his COVID-19 failure is a success," *Washington Post*, May 8, 2020, https://www.washingtonpost.com/outlook/2020/05/08/jared -kushner-coronavirus-failure/.

167 **"get enough credit"**: Philip Rucker, Josh Dawsey, Yasmeen Abutaleb, Robert Costa, and Lena H. Sun, "34 days of pandemic: Inside Trump's desperate attempts to reopen America," *Washington Post*, May 2, 2020, https://www.washingtonpost.com/politics/34 -days-of-pandemic-inside-trumps-desperate-attempts-to-reopen -america/2020/05/02/e99911f4-8b54-11ea-9dfd-990f9dcc71fc_story .html.

168 **"based on intuition"**: Grace Panetta, "'We have thrown 15 years of institutional learning out the window': Leaked emails show top public-health experts raised alarm about the Trump administration's botched coronavirus response," *Business Insider*, April 12, 2020, https://www.businessinsider.com/leaked-emails-show-experts-alarm -over-trump-admin-coronavirus-response-2020-4.

169 **"distractions, and denial"**: Jay Rosen, "The plan is to have no plan," PressThink, May 4, 2020, https://pressthink.org/2020/05 /the-plan-is-to-have-no-plan/.

169 **"John DiIulio, political science professor, University of Pennsylvania"**: Dan Balz, "Crisis exposes how America has hollowed out its government," *Washington Post*, May 16, 2020, https: //www.washingtonpost.com/graphics/2020/politics/government -hollowed-out-weaknesses/.

Chapter 8

171 **"Leona Helmsley"**: "Top 10 Tax Dodgers," *TIME*, https://content.time
.com/time/specials/packages/article/0,28804,1891335_1891333
_1891317,00.html.

171 **"Senator Tim Scott"**: Nnamdi Egwuonwu, "UAW president files
complaint against Tim Scott over 'you strike, you're fired' remark," NBC
News, September 22, 2023, https://www.nbcnews.com/politics/2024
-election/uaw-president-files-complaint-tim-scott-strike-re-fired
-remark-rcna116879.

172 **"stole the election"**: Jennifer Agiesta and Ariel Edwards-Levy,
"CNN Poll: Percentage of Republicans who think Biden's 2020 win
was illegitimate ticks back up near 70%," CNN, August 3, 2023,
https://www.cnn.com/2023/08/03/politics/cnn-poll-republicans
-think-2020-election-illegitimate/index.html.

172 **"such recession pessimism"**: Mark Zandi (@Markzandi), "In
my thirty plus years as a professional economist, I've never
seen such recession pessimism. But I've never seen such a
resilient economy. Something has to give. I suspect it will be the
pessimists," X (Twitter), May 14, 2023, https://x.com/Markzandi
/status/1657727082183393280?s=20.

174 **"two-thirds of US inflation"**: "Vox: America's inflation problem,
explained to the extent it is possible," American Economic Liberties
Project, March 28, 2022, https://www.economicliberties.us/media
/vox-americas-inflation-problem-explained-to-the-extent-it-is
-possible/.

175 **"not even close"**: "Shaefer testifies about the impact of the Child Tax
Credit before the U.S. House Select Subcommittee on the Coronavirus
Crisis," Ford School, University of Michigan, September 22, 2021,
https://fordschool.umich.edu/news/2021/shaefer-testifies-about
-impact-child-tax-credit-us-house-select-subcommittee-coronavirus
#:~:text=%E2%80%9CThis%20is%20the%20best%2C%20
most,the%20child%20tax%20credit%20permanent.

175 **"of Our Time"**: Daniel Henninger (@DanHenninger), "Spending Is
the Central Issue of Our Time by @DanHenninger https://wsj.com
/articles/spending-is-the-central-issue-of-our-time-mccarthy-debt
-deal-caps-reform-7b4cf49b?st=2muorkvenj7updj via @WSJopinion,"
X (Twitter), June 7, 2023, https://x.com/DanHenninger/status
/1666558532756422658?s=20.

176 **"and loan guarantees"**: Paul Krugman, "An Epidemic of Hardship
and Hunger," *New York Times*, May 7, 2020, https://www.nytimes
.com/202.0/05/07/opinion/coronavirus-republicans-jobs.html.

178 **"influence policy-makers"**: *NYT* Editorial Board, "Americans Pay a Price for Corporate Consolidation," *New York Times*, August 26, 3023, https://www.nytimes.com/2023/08/26/opinion/biden-lina-khan-ftc.html.

179 **"Black and Latino neighborhoods"**: Stacy Mitchell, "The Real Reason Your Groceries Are Getting So Expensive," *New York Times*, May 29, 2023, https://www.nytimes.com/2023/05/29/opinion/inflation-groceries-pricing-walmart.html.

179 **"leading up to it"**: Sheelah Kolhatkar, "Lina Khan's Battle to Rein in Big Tech," *New Yorker*, November 29, 2021, https://www.newyorker.com/magazine/2021/12/06/lina-khans-battle-to-rein-in-big-tech.

181 **"videos, and tweets"**: Robert Reich (@RBReich), "Remember: The explosion in CEO pay relative to the pay of average workers over the past few decades isn't because CEOs have become so much more valuable than before. They've just gamed the system to line their pockets," X (Twitter), September 15, 2023, https://x.com/RBReich/status/1702741027470090560?s=20

181 **"economist Thomas Piketty"**: *NYT* Editorial Board, "The Billionaires Are Getting Nervous," *New York Times*, November 8, 2019, https://www.nytimes.com/2019/11/08/opinion/sunday/bill-gates-warren-tax.html.

182 **"pay for civilization"**: *COMPANIA GENERAL DE TABACOS DE FILIPINAS v. COLLECTOR OF INTERNAL*, 275 U.S. 87 (1927), https://caselaw.findlaw.com/court/us-supreme-court/275/87.html.

185 **"members of the public"**: Noam Scheiber, "Amid Strikes, One Question: Are Employers Miscalculating?" *New York Times*, October 8, 2023, https://www.nytimes.com/2023/10/08/business/economy/labor-strikes.html.

188 **"self-reinforcing cycle"**: Peter Baker, "A Rising Tide Lifts Many Boats, but So Far Not Biden's," *New York Times*, August 4, 2023, https://www.nytimes.com/2023/08/04/us/politics/biden-approval-rating.html.

CONCLUSION

197 **"flight from reason"**: MSNBC (@MSNBC), "'The only way to fix the Republican party is to have it continue to lose,' Historian Jon Meacham says. 'I genuinely believe that it will be the ballot that convinces Republicans that they have to do something about this flight from reason,'" X (Twitter), August 20, 2023, https://twitter.com/MSNBC/status/1693243938138677549.

201 **"in death notices"**: Arlie Russell Hochschild, "How the White Working Class Is Being Destroyed," *New York Times*, March 17, 2020, https://www.nytimes.com/2020/03/17/books/review/deaths-of -despair-and-the-future-of-capitalism-anne-case-angus-deaton .html.

202 **"vision for America"**: "Trump's 2024 competition backs him against Maine ruling," MSNBC, December 29, 2023, https://www .msnbc.com/morning-joe/watch/trump-s-2024-competition-backs -him-against-maine-ruling-201092677997.

209 **"the attack wins"**: "Continuous Contact: Grant's Tactical Doctrine in the Eastern Theater," Emerging Civil War, August 4, 2020, https://emergingcivilwar.com/2020/08/04/continuous-contact -grants-tactical-doctrine-in-the-eastern-theater/#:-:text =%E2%80%9CIn%20every%20battle%20there%20comes,grand%20 tactic%20of%20Continuous%20Contact.

210 **"possibility of dictatorship"**: Robert Kagan, "A Trump dictatorship is increasingly inevitable. We should stop pretending," *Washington Post*, November 30, 2023, https://www.washingtonpost.com/opinions /2023/11/30/trump-dictator-2024-election-robert-kagan/.